CHRISTOPHER

Erec Edwards

Printed by Scriptron Production LLC, in the United States of America.

First Print: 10/2024

Scriptron Production LLC
115 Park Ave.
Bridgeport, CT 06604

http://novel.Scriptron.com

To dad, mom, brothers, and sister.

TABLE OF CONTENTS

Marsrise 11

Soulmates Forever 17

Fractured 21

Street Smarts 27

Weight of the Badge 33

Crimson Sector 36

Breaking Point 41

Smoke & Ash 46

The Storm 49

The Master Plan 52

Skyspire 55

Thin Line 59

General Greeley 62

Fork in the Road 65

Prototype 69

Shattered 73

Insurance 78

Blurred Lines 81

The Heart of a Machine 84

The Spear of Saar 88

Eyes on Me 92

Standoff 95

T.I.T.A.N. Unleashed 98

Torn the Heart Out 102

Flesh and Nanoceramic Steel 105

Lines Drawn 113

Fragile Alliance 118

Beneath the Flames 121

A Snowy Place 124

The Iron Gauntlet 127

Betrayal 130

The General's Gambit 133

Rebirth 137

One Final Mission 143

Epilogue 146

Appendix 148

Marsrise

New Sinai, Washington Quadrant, U.S. 2076 AD.

A.I.C.O. Northern Division

The A.I.C.O. (Artificial Intelligence Company) Northern Division dominated the industrial landscape of northern New Sinai, far from the civilian sectors. A massive complex of nanoceramic steel and carbonmatrix concrete, it resembled a fortress more than a corporate facility. No streets ran nearby, and no civilians wandered its sterile grounds. This was a place of pure function—machines, research, and security. The air hummed with the steady energy of the machinery that powered it, undisturbed by the usual bustle of city life.

Massive mirrored windows on the top floor reflected the pale light of a distant moon. The silence around the complex felt dense, almost oppressive, as if the entire structure held its breath. Then, in one violent instant, that silence shattered.

An explosion ripped through the top floor. The windows blew out, sending shards of glass, nanoceramic steel, and carbonmatrix concrete into the sky. The shockwave echoed across the complex, triggering alarms in every corner. Thick smoke billowed from the gaping wound in the building, and the mechanical hum faltered. Inside the A.I.C.O. hub, panic spread like wildfire.

~

Workers in protective suits scrambled through narrow hallways, shouting orders over the roar of fire and the wail of alarms—the once orderly facility descended into chaos. The sound of rushing footsteps, the clattering of tools, and the hum of malfunctioning systems filled the air.

In the robotics lab, destruction was absolute. Fires raged unchecked, devouring the remnants of advanced machinery. The orange glow from the flames swayed across broken consoles and shattered glass. Amid the wreckage, something stirred. Beneath twisted beams of metal, a figure began to rise, unnervingly calm.

His skin was untouched, smooth, and unscarred, as though the blast had torn apart the room around him but left him unharmed. His eyes, glowing a steady red, pierced through the smoke—cold and mechanical.

His engineers had named him Ares, but he called himself **Saar** (saw-HAR)—a cyborg, a construct built with purpose, for something far greater than the ruin surrounding him.

He stepped forward, moving deliberately over the rubble. Broken glass and jagged nanoceramic steel crunched underfoot, but he paid it no mind.

He paused at a malfunctioning communications console, its wiring sputtering with loose sparks. His finger shifted into a slender tool as he moved carefully, avoiding stray sparks. Messing with electricity wasn't part of the plan—not here, not ever. His tool slipped into the port, skillfully navigating the crackling energy around the console. The monitor flickered to life:

U.S. ARMY Network – Authorized Personnel Only. Access Granted!

Data streamed across the screen: protocols, maps, security clearances—until it all stopped on one line:

Project 24.

Saar's grip tightened on the console. He didn't need the entire file, just its location. His mission wasn't only about retrieval but about keeping a promise. With a flick, he severed the connection.

"Download complete. Location of Project 24 acquired. A.I.C.O. South," he muttered, his voice more machine than human.

Heavy footsteps echoed from the corridor. Saar froze, his head snapping toward the sound. Soldiers emerged at the far end, their tactical lights cutting through the smoke. Photon rifles were already trained on him.

In the dim light, Saar stood motionless, caught in the beam of their flashlights. Without hesitation, they opened fire. Bullets pinged harmlessly off his body, but he instinctively raised his arms to shield himself. His internal systems activated instantly, and his forearms shifted—not into deadly weapons, but non-lethal defenses: stun blasters and pulse disruptors. He moved faster than they could react, unleashing a pulse of energy that instantly dropped the soldiers to their knees. A second pulse followed, sending out debilitating sound waves that disoriented the entire squad.

Within moments, it was over. Every soldier lay incapacitated, but none were fatally harmed.

Saar knelt beside the soldier, watching his body jerk uncontrollably. The others had fallen still, but this one trembled, his chest heaving. Saar hesitated, his hand hovering just above the man's chest, frozen for a beat too long. His gaze flicked over the soldier's face, drawn to his breath's rapid rise and fall, the violent tremors that wouldn't stop. Saar blinked, his grip tightening for reasons he didn't fully understand.

Without a word, he released the nanobots from his arm. They flowed over the soldier's chest, quietly working to stabilize him. The convulsions eased, but Saar lingered, his hand still hovering. The feeling stayed with him, a weight that didn't lift, even as the soldier's breathing stabilized.

"You will live," Saar said.

He stood, quickly removing the uniform from one of the unconscious soldiers. The fabric fit him perfectly, as if tailored to his exact measurements. More footsteps echoed from the corridor—reinforcements were closing in. His focus sharpened.

In his mind, Saar called for her.

Zoe, find a way out!

Her response came as a thought, seamlessly blending with his own:

Calculating the optimal route, she responded, a voice only he could hear.

She was **ZOE**—short for Z.O.E.L., Zed Operative-Enhanced Logic. Calm, always there—a part of him. She wasn't just an A.I. There was something more, something deeper, as if she were woven into his very being. Her presence felt internal, almost instinctual, as though her voice had always been there, and he never questioned it.

Saar didn't need to understand how she worked—she just simply did. Her thoughts moved with his, guiding him through every situation with flawless accuracy. There was a strange comfort in her presence, as if she understood him beyond logic or data, a constant companion in a world that rarely made sense.

His vision flickered, and a digital overlay snapped into place across his mind, like a map etched onto the inside of his eyelids. The engineers had named it V.I.S.O.R.—Virtual Integrated Strategic Overlay & Response. Red markers lit up, pinpointing the soldiers' locations, while a glowing line traced the optimal escape route through the building. Zoe's calculations were never wrong.

I'll handle them. You lead me out, he ordered.

Acknowledged.

The soldiers advanced, but Saar was already moving. He disoriented them with another burst of energy, sending the squad staggering backward. His movements were fluid, evading their gunfire as he slipped into the stairwell.

He reached the landing and peered down the central shaft of the industrial complex. It plunged into the depths below—a vast, empty void. Flames licked along the nanoceramic steel framework, casting restless shadows on the descending walls. Something stirred inside him. A hesitation, unlike anything he'd felt before.

Is this the best way down? Saar asked.

Yes. Descent path calculated, Zoe said. *On launch, prepare for impact in ten-point-nine seconds.*

Saar halted at the edge, his grip tightening on the railing. The path flickered in his vision, mapped out with precision by Zoe, yet his body stalled, synthetic muscles tensing. He held there, unmoving, something off—something that shouldn't have been.

But, without further hesitation, he pushed off, launching himself into the void. The floors blurred as he dropped, Zoe's steady voice threading through his mind, but the tension clung to him, a weight that shouldn't be there, lingering all the way down.

Now, she said.

Saar's fingers clamped onto the metal support beams lining the shaft. Sparks flew as his synthetic grip slowed his descent, the screech of metal echoing as he slid down. His body was taut, each movement timed with perfect control.

Prepare for final deceleration, Zoe instructed.

Saar's grip tightened, sending another shower of sparks as the friction increased. He slowed to a near halt.

Release in three... two... one.

On cue, Saar let go, dropping the last few meters. His feet hit the ground with a heavy thud, the carbonmatrix concrete cracking beneath him. Smoke and sparks curled around his frame, but he stood unharmed, each movement as calculated as the last.

Descent complete.

Alarms blared up top as soldiers rushed down the stairwell, their boots pounding against the metal steps. But Saar was already several steps ahead.

With Zoe guiding him, he navigated the complex with unrelenting speed. His body moved with precision, taking sharp corners and bypassing security effortlessly. It was odd to him that this level had no security, unlike the ones above.

Each turn took him further from his pursuers until their shouts faded behind him. Saar vanished into the deeper corridors of the northern facility, leaving only wreckage and smoke in his wake.

~

Reaching a set of heavy metal doors, Saar kicked them open with a sharp blow, the nanoceramic steel groaning as it echoed down the halls. Outside, he paused at the edge of the complex, his glowing red eyes scanning the distant skyline of New Sinai to the south. The city's faint lights flickered beyond the maze of factories and nanoceramic steel.

For a moment, something flickered—a brief, unexplainable doubt. His systems ran a diagnostic, labeling it as a neural glitch. It had to be. He was built for accuracy, not feelings. Whatever it was, it was an error, and errors required correction. Without hesitation, Saar set off. His path was clear, his mission certain.

The city awaited.

Soulmates Forever

A few minutes before dawn, an explosion tore through the horizon of New Sinai, its light briefly chasing the night away. The sound followed—deep, rolling, shaking the bones of the megacity. The towering structures shuddered under the shockwave, glass and nanoceramic steel trembling. For a heartbeat, the city paused as though holding its breath. The blast wave struck the Grand Mass Church bell, causing it to resonate; its haunting tones lingered in the air. It felt like a bad omen.

~

In a quiet suburb, the light from the explosion flickered across polished surfaces. The tremor rattled windows, but the neighborhood remained undisturbed, save for one home.

~

Jay Mauritius stirred in bed, his body tense from the sudden vibration. Beside him, his wife Lillian slept, unmoved. He blinked, still caught between sleep and awareness.

"What...?"

He shifted closer to her, draping an arm over her protectively. Lillian, half-conscious, pushed his arm away with an absent motion. Soon, the house returned to its silence, and the disturbance outside faded into background noise.

By morning, sunlight cut through the last traces of the night. Lillian was already in the bathroom, the shower's soft hum filling the air. Jay stood in front of the bedroom mirror, dressed in his black police uniform, freshly shaved. His reflection stared back at him—stoic and composed, his LED BioVibe badge hung neatly on his chest, glowing with his name and badge number: 1936228.

His eyes drifted to the dresser, where framed photos of him and Lillian sat—smiling faces from a different era, when the world felt simpler—life before the silence grew louder between them. There were other photos, too—him with fellow officers, comradery frozen in time. Awards lined the walls, tokens of a career well-lived: commendations and trophies for bravery. But as he scanned his own memories, a hollowness settled in his chest.

He looked down at his hands. Rough and scarred, they felt like burnt burlap, weathered and hardened. The lines in his palms had all but disappeared, replaced by thick patches of calloused skin. The burns had taken more than just flesh—they had taken pieces of who he used to be. His hands trembled, and without warning, the memories of that day came flooding back—vivid and sharp, like it had just happened.

In his mind, he heard the crackle of fire, the groan of collapsing beams, and the scream—sharp, desperate, from a boy trapped inside. His hands shook harder. He closed his eyes, willing it to stop.

He took a deep breath and clenched his fists, forcing the tremors away. His reflection hardened, his face, a mask of control. There was no time for ghosts now. Without another glance at the mirror, Jay turned and left the room.

~

At the kitchen table, he and Lillian sat in silence. The clink of utensils was the only sound between them. She was focused on her HoloPad, scrolling steadily through headlines.

From the next room, the quiet hum of the house holoscreen—immersive images so real it felt like you were there—softly streamed the morning news:

> "Authorities confirmed that last night's explosion sent shockwaves through neighborhoods across New Sinai, shaking homes and shattering windows in the nearby districts. Officials are calling it an accident, with representatives from AICO assuring the public there is no risk of contamination. However, eyewitnesses report seeing black smoke billowing from the facility long after the

explosion, and local residents remain on edge, questioning the true extent of the damage."

Jay smirked faintly, shaking his head.

"Same script, different actors, huh?" Jay asked.

Lillian didn't look up, her attention still locked on her screen. He watched her momentarily, the silence between them heavy.

"You need a ride to work today?"

Lillian didn't look up. "No."

Her tone was flat, detached, as if the question barely registered. The silence that followed hung heavy between them. Jay shifted in his seat, fingers tapping the table, his mind grasping for words that wouldn't come.

"How about *from* work?"

"No need. Sarah's picking me up."

Another silence, deeper this time. Lillian sipped her coffee, still absorbed in her HoloPad.

"You're gonna be late," she said.

Jay forced a smile, though it didn't reach her eyes.

"If you want me gone, just say so."

For the first time that morning, her eyes met his, her face giving nothing away. Jay didn't need to ask. He pushed his chair back, the sharp scrape cutting through the quiet. He had almost reached the door when her voice caught him.

"You forgetting something?"

He glanced back, curious.

"Um… we don't kiss goodbye anymore," he said.

She held up his wedding ring, twirling it between her fingers.

"You left it in the bathroom. Again."

Jay blinked, then walked over. She handed the ring to him without breaking her focus on the HoloPad.

"Figured you might need it," she said.

He turned the ring over in his hand, reading the familiar inscription:

Jay & Lillian – Soulmates Forever.

"Forever's a long time, huh," Jay said, more to himself than to her.

The words were heavy, feeling almost absurd. Lillian looked up, her eyes briefly catching his. For a split second, there was something—maybe a reminder of what they once were. But it vanished just as fast, leaving behind the emptiness that had been growing between them for longer than either would admit.

Jay slid the ring back onto his finger, its presence feeling heavier than it used to, more like a weight than a symbol. It no longer felt like a promise, more like something he was carrying for the sake of it.

Lillian didn't respond. She simply stood up, gathering the plates, his and hers. Her face showed nothing, not a flicker of emotion. Each dish she picked up, each step she took, was like part of a routine she had performed a thousand times.

Jay hesitated; his gaze lingered on her, waiting for a sign—a glance, a word, anything. But nothing came. He exhaled quietly and turned away, heading for the door. It closed softly behind him, the gap between them feeling as permanent as ever.

Fractured

The highway was a mess. Hover hypercars idled a few inches from the ground, and magnetic transports sat in long single rows, stuck in place. Inside each vehicle, commuter faces told the same story as New Sinai: a frustration that simmered just below the surface.

So much for technology solving traffic.

Jay tapped his fingers on the console, his eyes flicking to the vehicle's holoscreen. The news anchor's voice cut through:

> "...While the nation celebrates its Tricentennial with large-scale events across the country, unrest continues closer to home. Protests have erupted locally in response to recent government remarks. The far-right group Fair Haven has criticized Quadrant Governor Bellwether's administration, accusing it of using the celebrations as a distraction from more pressing issues. Their grievances focus on job outsourcing, which they claim is causing widespread unemployment in the Washington Quadrant, along with unfair taxation policies. Additionally, the group argues that the local quadrant's spending lacks accountability, raising concerns about the transparency of the administration's budget."

On the screen, footage flickered between scenes of chaos—masked figures clashing with riot police, tear gas curling into the air, hypercars flipped and burning. New Sinai was crumbling before the cameras.

Jay shook his head. He remembered when the city had felt solid, like it could weather anything. Now, it barely held together like an old winter coat.

After a few grueling minutes, the traffic flowed smoothly again.

~

New Sinai stretched around Jay as he drove. Its carbonmatrix concrete, metal, and glass towers clawed at the sky. Beneath the layers of progress, the bones of Washington, D.C., still lingered for those who knew where to look. His eyes settled on the Washington Monument, now a faded shadow, dwarfed by the new skyline. The Lincoln Memorial's columns—cracked and patched repeatedly—stood as stubborn relics. No matter how often they were repaired, the fractures always returned, like the city's history refusing to heal. Jay kept driving, caught between the past and the present.

Hover hypercars zipped along in orderly, clean, and efficient lanes—at least when the traffic system felt like cooperating. Jay passed a cracked sign reading K Street. It meant something once, back when politics held the city together. Now, it was just another path through the decay. Buildings along the street sagged under the weight of time, their walls covered in layers of graffiti, each tag fighting for space with flickering ads projected into the air—holograms selling implants, immortality in digital form, vacations in virtual paradise—all fantasies for people who could never afford them.

Just above, police drones swept across the sky like mechanical vultures. They patrolled in tight, precise patterns, casting faint shadows over the streets below.

On clear nights, corporate logos took turns lighting up the moon, one after another, projected from the city below. Even the sky was no longer free.

He slowed at a red light, glancing out at the crowd. People moved through the streets like a slow river, weaving between flickering advertisements. Some looked human enough; others had more metal than flesh, limbs replaced with sleek prosthetics, their movements jerky and awkward. Jay's attention drifted to a vendor hunched by an alleyway, selling black-market parts near the old National Mall. The grandeur of that place was long gone, swallowed up by industrial parks and half-finished projects.

As he pressed the accelerator again, the weight of the city seemed to settle over him. New Sinai had been built on top of the ruins of Washington, yes, but it was no utopia. It was a patchwork of broken dreams held together by carbonmatrix concrete and nanoceramic steel. The cracks were everywhere— broken transport systems, flickering streetlights, and the slums hidden behind shiny new towers.

Ahead, the Grand Mass Church loomed over the skyline, a massive structure built where the Capitol once stood, now regarded as the dead center of the city. Its design was an odd blend of past and future, an attempt to unify the city's fractured spirit. Every night, the deep toll of The Peacemaker echoed like a warning. To some, it was a symbol of hope, but to Jay, it was just a reminder of how fragile everything had become.

The light turned green, and Jay pressed the pedal. The police station wasn't far, standing tall like a fortress against the city's chaos. As he drove into the underground garage, the city's weight seemed to lift, replaced by the sterile quiet within the station's walls. But no matter how deep he went, the tension of New Sinai was never far behind.

~

Minutes later, Jay stepped out of the garage and into the harsh atmosphere. The police headquarters loomed ahead, a towering structure of nanoceramic steel and glass, gleaming like a watchful sentinel over the city. Its sharp lines caught the midday sun, casting beams across the streets. Though its cold, fortified facade mirrored the skyline's grandeur, the building felt like a world apart—an island of order in a sea of urban chaos. Above, armed police drones circled silently, a constant reminder of the city's unyielding grip on control. Simultaneously, sleek patrol vehicles hovered several inches off the ground, silently, in and out of the underground garage; the hum of magnetic engines barely audible.

The entrance bustled with activity as uniformed and plain-clothed officers filtered through security checkpoints. Massive holoscreens flanked the doors, scrolling through the latest wanted lists and department bulletins.

~

Inside, the atmosphere was a different kind of intensity—cool, sterile, and meticulously organized. The walls were lined with seamless digital displays showing live feeds from surveillance drones and city-wide crime statistics. Officers moved purposefully through the polished corridors, their footfalls barely echoing on the sleek, black flooring. The air pulsed with the quiet hum of communication devices and the occasional chatter from holo-conferences.

In the heart of the building, the operations center brewed with activity, a massive control room where department analysts monitored the city in real-time, their eyes fixed on an endless grid of data streams and live video feeds. The building wasn't just a headquarters but the nerve center of New Sinai's order, looking more like a nuclear energy control room.

~

In the briefing room, Captain Bennett stood like a pillar of resolve, her stance commanding the space before she even spoke. Tall and broad-shouldered, she wore her perfectly pressed uniform like armor, every crease sharp, every detail precise. Her keen brown eyes swept across the room, speaking more than words as her voice cut through the air—calm, steady, and firm. She didn't need to shout; the weight of her presence alone held the room in silence.

But as her words filled the space, Jay's attention slipped, drawn instead to the blinking notification on the HoloPad in his lap.

> FROM: Dr. Timothy McCaffrey, Ph.D.
> SUBJECT: Urgent – Please Read
>
> Dear Officer Mauritius,
>
> After thoroughly reviewing your recent assessment, I must inform you that you've been diagnosed with Post-Traumatic Stress Disorder (PTSD), likely stemming from the traumatic experiences you've faced during your service. This condition may be affecting not only your mental health but

also your performance and decision-making in the line of duty.

It is imperative that you schedule a follow-up appointment as soon as possible to discuss a tailored treatment plan, which may include therapy, medication, or other supportive interventions. Your mental well-being is critical, and delaying care could lead to further complications. We strongly encourage you to take this step so that we can help you navigate the path to recovery and maintain your role effectively.

Sincerely,

Dr. Timothy McCaffrey, Ph.D.

Licensed Clinical Psychologist

The message hit Jay like a punch. His heart raced as he read the words over and over again: PTSD, treatment, mental health, performance. His chest tightened, the room around him fading as he stared at the screen.

Captain Bennett's voice broke through the fog.

"Officer Mauritius!"

Jay jolted upright.

"Yes, ma'am!"

"Anything you'd like to share with the rest of us?" she asked.

He hesitated.

"No, ma'am. Not really."

Her eyes stayed on him for a beat longer before she continued.

"Regarding last night's explosion," she continued, "at the industrial park, the U.S. Army had issued orders: no police presence at the site. The area is classified as restricted—no investigation, no interference, no anything! Understood?"

A wave of "Yes, ma'am" spread through the room, but Jay barely registered it. His hand clenched around the HoloPad, as if holding onto something solid might steady him.

Street Smarts

Now on police business, Jay's cruiser glided down the busy street, pausing at a red light. He glanced out the window, spotting the neon graffiti pulsing on a nearby wall.

Quadrant Chancellor = Quadrant Dictator

The colorful, bold letters shimmered briefly, a defiant challenge etched into the carbonmatrix concrete wall. Jay's gaze lingered before the light changed, and with a quiet sigh, he accelerated.

~

The cruiser sat quietly parked beyond the entrance of a neglected cemetery, where old headstones stood among digital ones, their screens flickering faintly in the shadows. Jay wandered through the rows, passing robot grave keepers that moved with mechanical precision, tending to the neglected stones.

He stopped before a weathered marker, its surface worn by time, and knelt to place a single white rose at its base. His fingers traced the name etched into the cold stone, lingering there with the reverence of someone left behind. In the distance, a low hum emanated from the grave keepers as they silently went about their tasks, indifferent to the grief around them.

The air seemed to grow heavier, his chest tightening as he lingered there, in silence. After a long breath, he pushed himself to his feet and walked back to the cruiser, the ache in his heart trailing behind him like a shadow.

Soon, the city's pulse quickly drew him back in.

~

Jay's police vehicle idled outside a small convenience store, one of the few relics of a simpler time. Inside, Roberto, the Puerto Rican owner, packed a bag for him with his usual care.

"I tossed in some extra bacon for you," Roberto said, in his thick Puerto Rican accent.

Jay gave a slight nod, appreciating the gesture. "Thanks," he said, reaching for the bag.

Roberto glanced out the window, shaking his head.

"Man, this city, verdad?" Roberto asked.

"Sorry, what?" Jay asked.

"This city! It's gettin' bad out there. Feels like the whole thing's fallin' apart, no?"

"Yeah, it's bad," Jay replied. "Protests on every corner, random blackouts... people are scared."

"I believe it. Too much chaos all at once. Feels like somebody's pullin' the strings. ¿Tú sabes? I heard about some weird checkpoints poppin' up in random places?"

"Checkpoints? No. That's news to me."

Roberto leaned against the counter, crossing his arms.

"The way things are goin', it wouldn't surprise me if New Sinai explodes like a piñata. You hear 'bout that explosion in the industrial park?"

"Of course. The Army's callin' it an accident, but..."

Roberto clicked his tongue, his expression serious.
"Siempre con los rumores, heh? It's funny. First, it's the protests, then terrorists, and now... who knows what. Every day, somethin' new, right?"

"Yeah. Rumors always make things worse," Jay said before changing the subject. "You staying safe?"

Roberto waved his hand dismissively.
"Safe? As safe as I can be, hermano. This place is too small for anyone to notice, but you never know." He tapped the counter lightly, then leaned down, revealing the barrel of a shotgun resting just below it. "See this? Just in case."

"Hey. Be careful with that."

"Sí, always," he said as he straightened up, "One good blast from that, and anyone thinkin' they can mess with me or my shop, will think twice. I'm just hopin' this craziness blows over soon. But, if not, I'm ready—por si acaso."

"Alright," Jay said as he walked away. "Stay sharp, Roberto."

"You too, hermano. Don't let this city get to you. ¡Cuídate!"

The door hissed shut behind him.

~

The marketplace buzzed with chaotic energy as Jay moved through it. Holographic signs floated above the stalls, hawking cheap gadgets and imitation goods. The voices of human and artificial vendors merged into an unintelligible cacophony, but Jay pressed on, navigating through the crowd of bodies—both natural and synthetic—with practiced ease.

Above him, the familiar police drones hovered in their usual patrol patterns, their small frames barely noticeable to anyone used to life in New Sinai. But something larger loomed further up, casting a faint shadow over the stalls. Jay's eyes caught it—a drone far bigger than the standard patrol models, sleek and unfamiliar.

Jay frowned, his eyes following the larger drone as it drifted into the haze. It wasn't one of theirs —that much he knew. Too big, too quiet, and definitely not standard issue. He wasn't sure if it was just some new tech being tested or if it had a different purpose altogether, but one thing was clear: whatever it was doing here, it wasn't routine.

His grip tightened on the bag as he made his way toward the quieter edges of the market, eyes scanning the faces around him. He was looking for someone and knew he would be somewhere away from the noise and the chaos.

Near the fringes, past the neon haze, Andre sat on a threadbare blanket. His gaunt frame and ragged clothes made him easy to overlook, sitting away from everyone and everything, like tossed garbage in the city's forgotten corners. But Andre was always present—part of the city's fabric in a way only those paying attention would notice. His dog Diggity, a female Golden Retriever, was comfortably curled beside him.

Jay's approach drew a faint smile to his broken face, a brief spark of warmth in a life that offered little.

"Andre!" Jay shouted.

"Jay! My man!" Andre said, sitting up straighter.

Jay crouched to greet Diggity, her tail wagging furiously.

"She still likes me more than you," Jay said.

Andre laughed, teeth crooked but sincere.

"She'll love anyone with bacon stuffed in their pockets."

Jay chuckled and handed him the bag.

"Dinner and breakfast. In case I don't make it by tonight."

Andre peeked inside, his expression softening.

"You don't have to do this, Jay. You know that."

"I know that."

Andre handed a strip of bacon to Diggity, who eagerly devoured it before he took a bite himself.

"You get me coffee?"

"Yeah. In the bag."

"Good man!" Andre said.

Jay tried to hand him bottled water, but Andre refused it in disgust.

"Bottled water's the devil's piss, man," he said through a mouthful of sandwich.

"Here we go again," Jay said.

"They dose it with chemicals. Tryin' to sterilize all of us."

"No, they're not!"

"They're tryin' to neuter us. All of us!"

Jay raised an eyebrow.

"You know the coffee's made with water, right?"

Andre paused, chewing thoughtfully.

"Yeah… but… the caffeine neutralizes the chemicals."

Jay shook his head, a smirk tugging at his lips. Andre's face grew more serious.

"I'm telling you, Jay, they're behind it all—the flu outbreaks, for instance. The government tweaks the virus every so often so they can sell new versions of the vaccine every other year. Keeps the cash cow alive."

Jay sighed softly, playing along.

"You might be right."

A pause settled between them.

"Have you thought about what we discussed?" Jay asked.

Andre hesitated, feeding Diggity another piece of bacon.

"Still thinkin'."

"Winter's coming, Andre. It's gonna be rough. You can't stay out here."

Andre looked away. Jay saw it in his eyes before he pulled back—the worry, the unspoken fear.

"I can take you to the Grand Mass Church," Jay said. "It's only a few minutes away. They've got space. It's not permanent, but it'll get you off the streets. For now."

Andre recoiled, shaking his head.

"Hell no! No way! I'm not stepping foot in that place of evil."

"Why not?"

"I hear that's where they harvest people's organs. While you sleep, no less! You wake up missin' a kidney, a spleen, or worse, your brain!"

Jay stared at him, trying to gauge how serious he was.

"That's the most ridiculous thing I've ever heard! They're there to help."

"Yeah. Help you die!" His voice was tinged with paranoia.

Jay sighed, pulling a few e-bits from his pocket and dropping them into Andre's cup, already brimming with spare change. Andre shot him a grateful glance.

"You don't trust bottled water," Jay said, "you don't trust the church, but yet, you'll money without question?"

"Hey, I don't make the rules."

"You make absolutely no sense," Jay said.

He ruffled Diggity's fur one last time, then turned to Andre.

"I'll see you tomorrow. Maybe."

Andre's eyes sparkled mischievously.

"Just remember, Jay—drink too much of that bottled water, and your nuts'll explode."

Jay shook his head, laughing as he waved goodbye, his steps fading into the crowded market, leaving Andre's laughter to echo in the distance.

Weight of the Badge

Jay eased his cruiser into the shadowed alleyway, the glow of distant fires reflecting in his rearview mirror. The protests had been relentless for weeks, the city teetering on the edge, and tonight wasn't improving.

The radio crackled to life, dispatch flooding in with more calls than Jay had time to process. He gestured for the volume to lower, needing a moment to focus as he surveyed the scene ahead.

A small group of looters had gathered around a shattered storefront, stuffing electronics into black duffel bags. They moved quickly, eyes darting nervously toward the street.

Above them, a surveillance drone hovered; its red light blinked steadily as it recorded everything. Jay knew it had already sent an alert to the precinct—these days, the drones were faster at reporting crimes than any human witness could ever be. Quiet eyes in the sky, they patrolled the city in constant, watchful sweeps, always calling in the trouble before he'd arrived. Despite that, looters didn't care at all. They expected the police to arrive in seconds, not minutes.

Jay sighed, rubbing his temples. "Of course," he muttered.

It was the same story, over and over—people driven by desperation, making choices they couldn't take back. He reported the situation, though he knew the drone had already captured most of the details. As he stepped out of the hypercar, the weight of his badge seemed heavier than usual.

The group scattered when his boots hit the pavement, vanishing into the alleys like shadows. In a split second, one kid froze in hesitation, and that's all it took for Jay to spring into action and dash after him.

The alley was narrow; the boy was fast, but not fast enough. Jay's belt rattled with the weight of his gear as he ran, each piece of equipment banging against him louder with every stride. It all felt heavier now, almost dragging him down. The handcuffs on his belt rattled, and his breath became sharper, each step more burdened by the noise and weight of everything he carried. Still, he kept up, his focus locked on the boy.

Jay reached out, grabbing the back of the kid's jacket and pulling him to the ground.

"Don't move," Jay ordered, holding the kid down.

The boy fought hard, flailing wildly, like a trapped animal.

"Stop! I'm not gonna hurt you," Jay said, loosening his grip.

The kid went still, his chest heaving. Jay didn't cuff him—there was no point. He was too young, too scared, eyes wide with the kind of fear that came from realizing you'd already lost. Dirt and tears streaked down his face, mixing into muddy lines. For a moment, Jay just stared at him, seeing more than just a looter—seeing the desperation, the same kind of helplessness he'd once felt at that age.

Jay helped the boy to his feet as the drone hovered at a safe distance above, recording everything. Jay glanced up at it, an idea forming. He needed to help the kid, but the drone was always watching, feeding footage directly into the city's permanent archive.

"Walk," Jay said, guiding the boy toward the cruiser.

The kid stayed quiet, but Jay could feel his fear. He glanced at the drone again, then down at the cuffs hanging from his belt. He had to trick the system and find a way to throw off those ever-watchful digital eyes.

"What's your name, kid?" Jay asked.

The boy didn't respond, his head hanging low. Jay didn't press, slowing his steps as they neared the cruiser, buying himself some time. The drone lingered above, patient and tireless.

Jay paused by the hypercar, pretending to check something on his boot. As he did, he slipped the cuff key into his palm, even though he wasn't planning to use it. Standing, he surveyed the surroundings, looking for anything that might help break the drone's line of sight—a tree, a signpost, anything.

"You're gonna do exactly what I say," Jay whispered. "When I open the back door, you run. Got it?"

The boy's eyes widened, but he didn't argue. Jay opened the back door, using the cruiser itself as cover. He shifted his body and the door just enough to keep the drone's view partially blocked.

For a few precious seconds, Jay was sure the drone couldn't catch anything suspicious. He gave the kid a quick nod.

The boy took off. Jay stayed by the hypercar, making small adjustments to keep the door in the drone's line of sight, acting like nothing was wrong. He watched the boy disappear into the shadows, confident that the drone hadn't captured a thing.

After a few moments, Jay called it in.

"Suspect resisted arrest. Got away into the alleys." He wiped a hand over his face, the gravity of what he'd done settling in.

He knew it wasn't a solution. But for tonight, he'd given the kid another chance. Maybe a kid like him deserved it.

Jay couldn't help but think back to his own days, running from cops in alleys just like this. Stealing to survive had been a necessity back then, and he knew exactly what that fear felt like—the fear of being caught, of a future you couldn't see beyond the next day. He got out of that life, barely. But if things had gone just a little differently, he'd be the one locked up or worse.

His radio crackled again, and dispatch was already sending him to the next crisis. Jay climbed into the cruiser, catching a glimpse of the drone still floating above.

No rest for the weary.

Crimson Sector

Mama Bear's Lounge stood like an aging monument to the city's forgotten vices in the Crimson Sector, a beacon of neon lights pulling in anyone who wandered too close, eager for their time and e-bits. Above the door, a holographic projection looped endlessly—dancers moving with fluid precision, their bodies too perfect to be real. Below, people paused, spellbound for a moment before either turning away or disappearing inside, lured by the muffled throb of the music seeping through the walls.

~

Inside, the atmosphere buzzed with energy. The music's pulse wasn't just something you heard; it was something you felt, reverberating through your chest and settling deep in your hips and loins. New sound wave technology teased your senses, like butter in the air of a movie theater, but this time it touched every part of you, right down to your most primal urges.

On the stage, performers—some fully human, others enhanced with cybernetic limbs—moved in harmony with holograms of dancers. The blend of flesh and tech was so seamless that it felt like they existed in the same world, a blur of movements that made you question where the organic ended and the synthetic began. Eyes were glued to the spectacle, patrons gripping their drinks as though letting go would break the spell.

Jay sat at the bar, absentmindedly twisting his wedding ring as the neon glow of the club flickered in the background. He barely noticed the music or the movement of the performers—the noise was distant, like a murmur beneath his real thoughts.

Beside him, Grier and Diaz, Jay's closest friends, both off-duty officers, were already in the middle of one of their usual arguments.

"You're out of your damn mind," Grier snapped, his voice louder than needed. "The Quadrant system was a disaster from day one."

"I'm not saying it was great," Diaz replied, "but it's the only reason we're even sitting here. What else could we have done? Let the country fall apart while the war swallowed us whole?"

Jay glanced between the two, his hand still on his drink, eyes flickering over the rim of his glass.

"Saved us?" Grier scoffed. "All it did was hand the country over to a pack of corrupt chancellors. That's why we're in this mess now! They're pulling the strings, not the Office of States or even the President. And don't get me started on that Director. Man, would I love to reboot his face!"

Diaz's cybernetic fingers drummed against the bar in frustration.

"You've got it all backward, Grier," he said. "The Office of the States was the safeguard. The Director reports straight to the President. They are the only ones keeping the quadrants from becoming fiefdoms."

Jay sighed, sensing this was about to boil over. "Keeping them in check?" Grier's jaw clenched. "Really? Look around, man. The Washington Quadrant's a disaster. New Sinai's just a pile of junk with neon lights slapped on top of it. Those chancellors? They've done nothing but suck the life out of us." "You're not seeing the big picture. If we didn't have the quadrant system, we'd still be in the middle of a war. The country wouldn't exist anymore. The chancellors may not be saints, but without them, we'd have chaos." "You call this order?" Grier said. "Drones overhead, ads blasted into the goddamn clouds, noise day and night—this is your idea of peace?" "It's better than living through gunfire and riots every day!" "That's where you're wrong." Jay finally spoke up, cutting through the argument. They turned to look at him, surprised to see him join in. Jay sat up, his voice steady, calm but firm. "Diaz, you're missing the point. The quadrant system didn't save us. It patched things up, sure, but it's not a real fix. Grier's right about one thing—the chancellors were given too much power. Congress thought creating those offices would stabilize things, but all they did was split the country in a whole different way. Into pieces." Diaz opened his mouth to respond, but Jay held up a hand, stopping him. "I'm not saying the Office of the States didn't have a role, but let's not pretend they've kept the chancellors on a leash. The Director reports to the President, yeah, but the hell is the President? A figurehead? No. The real power lies with the quadrants now. The Chancellors." Grier crossed his arms, satisfied that Jay was backing him up. "Exactly. That's what I've been saying." "But don't think you've got the whole story, either," Jay said. "You're acting like the quadrant system is the root of all our problems. It's not. The collapse started long before that. The war tore the country apart; the quadrant system was the only thing left standing in the aftermath. If we didn't have that, we'd be in ruins—no cities, no laws, nothing. We would be back in the dark ages." Both of them fell silent, listening now. "The war didn't just stay on battlefields," Jay continued. "It flooded into every street, every home. I was only a kid, but I remember it. Families were torn apart, cities were burning, and everything was crumbling around us. When it ended, the states were barely holding on. The quadrants were supposed to be a solution, but they were a compromise—one we've never really recovered from."He leaned back, taking a sip from his glass. "Yeah, it's a mess, but it's our mess now." The three sat there in silence for a while, the noise of the bar filling the space between them. It wasn't a resolution, but it was enough for the moment.

Hours slipped by, and Grier and Diaz finally staggered out, too drunk to keep arguing. Jay stayed behind, still perched on his stool, spinning his wedding ring without thinking. His gaze fixed on the empty glass in front of him. He signaled for another drink without a glance, his mind far removed from the noise and lights around him.

Patrons flowed in and out, but to Jay, they were just blurred shapes passing by. He drained his glass, stood up with a wobble, and staggered toward the exit. Heading home.

~

The cool night air hit him like a bitch slap, but it wasn't enough to clear his head. His thoughts were thick, his limbs sluggish. The streets swayed in his alcohol-induced vision, and the figures around him drifted like ghosts. He fumbled with his watch, summoning his hypercar, and heard the faint beep as it approached from the distance.

Sliding into the driver's seat, Jay struggled with the controls. The engine purred beneath him, but he barely noticed. His eyes fluttered shut almost instantly, and sleep took over, pulling him into a deep, booze-soaked oblivion.

Sometime later, the sharp blare of hypercar horns cut through his haze, followed by a knock on the window. Jay jerked awake, his face pressed awkwardly against the wheel. Disoriented, he wiped away a bit of drool, trying to gather himself. The knock came again, harder this time.

Jay squinted through the glass, barely able to make out the figure of a fellow police officer. He hit the button to lower the window, his words stumbling out, slow and slurred, blending together.

"Whaz-zit? Can I help you, off'sir?"

The officer's face showed no patience, his expression flat with irritation.

"Move your vehicle! Right now!"

Jay blinked, his brain struggling to process.

"My... wha' now?"

"Your vehicle, move it!"

Jay's thoughts dragged, the alcohol still thick in his veins.

"No... y'don't... you don't understand..."

"Have you been drinking?"

"Me? Naaaaaah," Jay replied, laughing at the absurdity.

The officer's tone sharpened.

"I said, move your vehicle. I won't ask again."

Jay waved him off lazily.

"C'mon, "c'mon, man. I'm... I'm a cop, too. Jus' needed to close my eyes... f'like, f'like a sec."

"I don't care if you're the Space Pope."

Jay's mind was slow to absorb the insult.

"Heeeeeey, man... no need to be... be all hostile. I jus' parked... parked here f'a minute."

"Sir! You are parked in the middle of the goddamn intersection!"

The officer snapped, jabbing a finger at the scene.

Jay slowly turned his head, the slight movement feeling monumental. His hypercar sat in the middle of the intersection, with traffic weaving around it and angry horns blaring from every direction.

It took Jay a few seconds to grasp the situation.

"Oh."

Breaking Point

Jay rested beside his wife, the soft glow from his HoloPad casting pale light across the room. Wrapped in blankets, Lillian slept quietly, her breathing steady. The silence in the room felt thin, like a fragile bubble in a world always ready to burst. But quiet moments never lasted.

A brilliant flash of orange split the night, lighting the room in harsh, stinging brightness. Seconds later, a shockwave hit, shaking the windows and rattling the walls. The bed trembled beneath them. Lillian stirred, half awake, her words muffled by sleep.

"I wasn't snoring," she muttered.

Jay didn't respond. He was already moving, his HoloPad thudding to the floor as he shot out of bed. His body, too familiar with emergencies, acted without thinking. He pulled the curtains back and saw the flames lighting up the horizon.

It's close to the market. Too close.

His training kicked in. This wasn't just an accident. His phone buzzed on the nightstand. He picked it up, answering immediately. The voice on the other end was tense.

"Governor's orders. Full lockdown. The captain wants you in."

Jay paused, the gravity of the moment settling over him.

"Yeah. I'm on my way."

He stood still after the call, his mind catching up to the reality of what was happening. Without a second thought, he grabbed the remote and switched on the holoscreen; the images felt as if he were right in the middle of them. The screen was filled with images of chaos—fires eating away at hypercars, storefronts shattered, and people scattered in every direction.

One scene stopped him in his tracks—a *lone soldier* fighting the police and military.

The newscaster's voice broke through the noise:

> "Breaking news from New Sinai, where protests by Fair Haven opposition groups have erupted into full-scale riots. What began as a series of peaceful demonstrations has now escalated into widespread violence. Reports indicate extensive looting and arson throughout the downtown districts, with several key buildings already engulfed in flames. Law enforcement is struggling to maintain control as clashes between protesters and police have become increasingly hostile. Numerous attacks on police officers have been confirmed, some resulting in serious injuries.
>
> In response to the escalating unrest, the state governor has declared a state of emergency and imposed a strict, city-wide curfew. Effective immediately, all civilians are ordered to stay indoors. Anyone found on the streets without proper clearance will be detained on sight. Authorities warn that further unrest will not be tolerated, and additional security forces are being deployed to key locations throughout the city.
>
> This situation continues to develop as tensions rise between New Sinai and the Fair Haven opposition. Stay tuned for updates as we bring you the latest from this rapidly unfolding crisis."

The screen shifted to a massive blaze, the flames so intense it felt like the heat might reach out to him. Jay's breath caught. He wasn't watching anymore; he was there. He could feel the heat, smell the burning debris, hear the crackle of flames. His hands throbbed—old scars aching with memory.

A scream echoed in his mind. A boy's scream. Jay blinked hard, but the image wouldn't leave—a child huddled under a blanket, eyes wide with terror as the fire closed in.

Jay clenched his fists, forcing the memory downward. When he opened his eyes, the room was quiet again. The holoscreen droned on, but it felt distant.

Lillian was standing now, watching him from the side of the bed, concern etched into her face.

"You alright?" she asked softly.

Jay exhaled, steadying himself.

"Yeah. Fine."

"What's going on?"

"Curfew. I've been called in."

He walked toward the closet, but her hand caught his arm, stopping him.

"I meant with you."

Jay didn't reply, gently pulling away as he grabbed his uniform. The fabric felt heavier than usual as he dressed, avoiding her gaze. Lillian sat on the bed, watching him in silence.

"It's always something, isn't it?" she said quietly.

Jay glanced at the mirror. His reflection looked tired.

"Yeah. That's the job."

He started toward the door, but her voice stopped him, again.

"*I meant*, between us."

The words lingered in the air, heavy with meaning. She hesitated before speaking again.

"I don't think this is working anymore," she said, her voice shaking.

Jay froze, a tightness forming in his chest.

"What?!"

"Maybe… we should see other people."

Her words hit like a punch, leaving him breathless. He turned to face her, confusion and disbelief mixing on his face.

"You're bringing this up now?! In the middle of the night?! With the city falling apart?!"

"When else am I supposed to bring it up?!" she said. "You're never here. You're always out… there, or lost in your own head. You don't see what's happening to us!"

Tears welled up in her eyes.

"Is it me? Am I not enough for you anymore? Do I need implants? Maybe some fancy mechanical butt?"

Jay stayed silent. He wanted to say something, anything, but the words wouldn't come.

"Are you seeing someone else?" she asked.

"No!" He said instantly.

"I have an emergency, Jay. Why can't you just be here? I need you right now."

The silence that followed was unbearable. Lillian's voice softened to almost nothing.

"I still love you." Lillian continued, "But you've been different since we…"

Her voice trailed off, but Jay knew exactly what she meant.

"Lost your baby?" He said.

"Lost *our* baby!" she corrected, her voice raw with pain.

Jay flinched, the mention of it reopening an old wound he had been trying to forget. The future they had imagined was gone, replaced by an emptiness neither could fill. They couldn't face what they had lost together. When he finally spoke, his voice was a whisper.

"I can't do this right now."

Her eyes filled with tears again.

"No shit. You never can, can you?" she said. "You're just incapable."

She didn't wait for a response. She turned and walked into the bathroom, slamming the door behind her.

Jay stood there, feeling her words weigh down on him. Her muffled sobs echoed through the closed door, and he felt hollow. With nothing left to hold onto, he turned and walked away.

Smoke & Ash

It was close to midnight, and the horizon glowed a harsh, fiery orange. Street fires flickered across the city, casting jagged shadows on the walls and pavements, the flames twisting into unpredictable shapes. The smoke drifted, slow and thick, carrying the bitter stench of burning as it blurred the skyline. Above the rooftops, sharp red laser beams pierced the haze, scrawling a blunt warning across the clouds, a message no one could possibly miss:

Military Order: Immediate Curfew. All citizens must be inside by 10 PM.

As Jay neared the police station, he paused, taking in the surreal scene before him—chaos surrounded like a moving surreal painting. Flames licked at the edges of buildings; broken windows reflected the firelight, and the distant crack of gunshots echoed through the night air. His heart raced at the sound, snapping him out of the moment. The city wasn't just on fire but unraveling like ripped fabric. He muttered a curse under his breath and quickened his steps.

~

Inside New Sinai's police station, the atmosphere felt suffocating. The tension buzzed like static, hanging heavy. Officers moved with grim purpose, their faces drawn tight, their eyes dulled by exhaustion and the weight of what was happening outside. It felt less like a police station and more like a bunker, barely holding the line between order and collapse.

Jay weaved through the crowded room, scanning the faces until he saw Captain Bennett. She cut through the noise with the kind of determination only exhaustion could sharpen. He couldn't let her disappear into the chaos without getting answers.

"Captain!" Jay called, falling into step beside her. "What do you have?"

Bennett didn't stop. Her voice was sharp, matching her pace.

"Protesters, armed to the teeth. They're shooting at us, the National Guard, and the Army."

"Army?" Jay wasn't surprised easily, but that caught him off guard.

"Yeah," she said with a nod. "The Mayor called us first. The Governor brought in the National Guard, and now the Chancellor has sent the Army to back everyone up. It's a full-scale mobilization."

Jay frowned, his gut telling him something wasn't adding up.

"This doesn't make sense. All this for protesters?"

Bennett paused, just long enough to look him in the eye.

"You're asking the wrong person. But there's more—something you need to hear."

Jay's stomach dropped.

What now?

"Internal Affairs," she said. "They've been sniffing around since last night. And there's talk about you letting a suspect free, you being parked in the middle of an intersection. Some kind of health issue?"

Jay's chest tightened.

Her expression softened—something Jay wasn't used to seeing from her.

"They didn't get into details," she replied, "Look, I'm on your frequency, but for now, you've got to outthink this. I'm keeping you off anything that might land you in a deeper mess."

"What are you saying?"

"Stick to the basics. Patrols, rounding up curfew breakers, chasing looters—nothing that'll make you a target. No heroics. No unnecessary risks. Just keep your head down and follow orders. Got it?"

Jay nodded slowly, his mind already racing.

"Got it."

Bennett gave him a quick nod before disappearing into the sea of stressed-out officers. Jay stood there for a moment, letting it all sink in. Something was off. He could feel it in his bones. But for now, orders were orders.

The Storm

Jay gripped the wheel; his knuckles pale against the steering column as the cruiser tore through the shattered streets. The radio crackled with chaotic chatter—calls blurring into one another, barely audible over his heart pounding. He had to reach the marketplace. Fast!

The cruiser dodged abandoned hypercars and debris, weaving through wreckage as smoke thickened. The wreckage wasn't just scattered junk—it was the ruins left behind by a full-scale war. The glow of distant flames flickered against the night, marking his destination, the marketplace. Once the heart of the district—now looked like a warzone. Jay's gut clenched. His foot pressed harder on the gas.

~

As he closed in, the scene grew worse. Stalls that had once overflowed with food and goods were nothing but twisted metal and glowing embers. Black smoke curled into the sky, thick and acrid, blotting out the stars.

The remnants of a violent clash lay scattered across the market. Soldiers from the U.S. Army—their bodies motionless but not dead—were slumped near toppled vehicles. Jay could feel the faint hum of energy—plasma blasts, judging by the scorched craters in the ground. Everything within the blast radius had been roasted.

Jay scanned the area, frustration tightening. The soldiers were unconscious, their weapons discarded and useless. He couldn't ask what had happened—there were no answers here, no signs of life.

Citizens had vanished without a trace, and not a single police officer was found, dead or alive.

Reaching for his radio, he hesitated. Calling for an ambulance was pointless. Every emergency service was drowning under the chaos that had swallowed the city. Help wasn't coming, not tonight.

He slammed on the brakes, skidding to a stop, and flung the hypercar door open. His boots hit the ground hard as he sprinted forward, eyes scanning. His voice cracked out of him, desperate.

"Andre," he called, starting quietly before shouting louder. "Andre!"

Nothing.

And then, through the haze, movement—a dog, tied to a post, trembling. He felt a flicker of hope.

"Diggity!" he called, running over.

The dog whined, her tail barely wagging as she recognized him. Jay knelt beside her, gently combing his fingers through her fur, checking for injuries. She was unharmed but frightened.

Jay's eyes shifted to where Andre's makeshift stall had once stood. Now it was empty, his belongings scattered. Just beyond, a dark stain marked the ground— blood. His gut twisted.

No.

He crouched, fingers brushing the dried red. It was fresh. Andre had been here or someone else. Whoever tore through this place had taken him. Or worse. With urgency burning in his chest, Jay untied Diggity, speaking softly.

"Come on, girl."

~

The inside of the convenience store was dim; the emergency lights cast long shadows over the narrow aisles. The windows had been shuttered, the only barrier between the chaos outside and the fragile silence within. A loud banging on the door shattered that silence.

Behind the counter, Roberto's hands trembled around the shotgun, his eyes darting toward the entrance.

"I got a gun!" he shouted, voice shaking. "I got a gun!"

A muffled reply. "Roberto! It's me! Jay! Officer Mauritius!"

Roberto exhaled in relief, peeking through the narrow slit in the gate before unlocking the door. Jay slipped inside quickly.

"Qué bueno verte, hermano," Roberto said, still gripping the shotgun tightly. "I thought you were the looters. Or worse. It's crazy out there—trucks, guns, Army! Everything!"

Jay's eyes wandered around the store, taking in the cramped space and Roberto's nervous energy. Roberto shifted under his gaze, the weight of everything outside pressing him.

"You're gonna take me home, right?" Roberto asked.

"No, man. You're safer here. Curfew's in effect. If you're caught outside, you'll get locked up."

Jay led Diggity over and handed Roberto the leash. The dog looked up at Jay, then at the stranger, confused.

"Take care of her," Jay said. "Her name's Diggity. I'll come back for her." He slipped e-bits into Roberto's hand. "She loves bacon."

Roberto nodded, unsure but compliant, gripping the leash. Behind him, Diggity let out a low, sad whine. Jay turned toward the door.

"Where are you going?" Roberto asked.

Jay paused for a second, glancing back at the dog, then at Roberto.

"I have to find her owner."

The Master Plan

Jay hadn't heard the sounds of war since he was a kid, back when the fighting was just far-off thunder. Now, it was right on his doorstep. He eased his cruiser to a stop at a sprawling intersection. The road was littered with debris and makeshift barricades that blocked his path. Squinting through the haze, he tried to make sense of the wreckage ahead. The destruction that tore through the marketplace had swept through here, too, leaving nothing but chaos. This place wasn't safe.

He muttered a curse under his breath and pushed the door open. The night air, cool but tinged with ash, hit him.

Overhead, six drones zipped by, engines buzzing as they sped toward the conflict. Jay recognized the design of the drones from earlier in the marketplace.

They're military.

Every fiber in Jay urged him to turn back, to leave it all behind. He turned to go, but something stopped him in his tracks.

Don't get involved. Just walk away.

A nearby explosion lit up the intersection, bright as a flash of dawn. The ground shook, and the echo rumbled down the empty streets like distant thunder.

The weight of the moment dragged at his shoulders. Whether it was a sense of duty or morbid curiosity, he couldn't tell. His eyes fell tothe old service revolver on his hip. He pulled it out, the cold metal feeling heavier than ever—a reminder of what crossing this line would truly mean.

"Damn."

He stepped forward, moving into the intersection and toward the heart of the district.

~

Ahead, the intersection was locked down, jammed with abandoned hypercars and makeshift blockades. National Guard and Army soldiers crouched behind the barriers, photon rifles aimed at the metro hub just a few hundred feet away—no sign of the police. Not a word was spoken. An uneasy stillness hung over everything, as if the entire scene held its breath.

Jay crouched behind a burned-out shell of a hypercar, keeping his breath steady, careful to stay out of sight. Adrenaline heightened his senses as he scanned the scene, his eyes darting across the landscape.

~

The metro hub loomed, a hulking carbonmatrix concrete structure that once bustled with hovering taxis, buses, and other civilian transports. Now, it sat eerily still. Beyond it, the Skyspire towered a few hundred feet into the sky, bristling with satellite dishes and lights like a menacing, twisted Christmas tree. It overlooked the hub, like Goliath over David, its presence casting a long, unshakable shadow. For a moment, Jay thought he could hear the faint hum of its electronics breaking through the stillness.

Suddenly, an engine roared, tearing through the artificial stillness. A TALON—Tactical Assault Land Operations Neutralizer, a large, rugged, and versatile military vehicle—skidded into view, tires screeching as it spun and slammed to a stop. Built to seat up to six soldiers, the vehicle's headlights pierced through the swirling dust and debris, cutting sharp beams into the disarray ahead. Instantly, spotlights from the barricades and hovering Army drones snapped onto it, flooding it with harsh light.

Jay tensed. He didn't know what to make of it yet. Before he could think, three more Talons rolled into view, their engines growling as they formed a tight circle around the first. Mounted on top of each were heavy .50-caliber machine guns, their barrels trained on the trapped vehicle. Soldiers dressed in black uniforms jumped out, weapons ready, their movements precise and practiced. They were the 13th Ghost Battalion, U.S. Special Forces.

Among them stood one man who seemed to command the scene without effort. Commander Acer Nathaniel Wayne, or Commander Acer, moved with sharp, deliberate confidence, like the ground bent to his will. His rigid posture wasn't from fatigue—it was the kind of certainty that came from never having his authority questioned. His face, marked by conflict, held the relaxed confidence of a man who believed every victory was his doing. His jaw clenched with the tension of someone who expected nothing but obedience.

"We've got him, sir," one of his soldiers said.

"No shit," Acer said.

His gaze swept the scene. He took his time before responding, not one to rush. Too many things went wrong when people rushed.

He snapped his fingers. "Bullhorn. Bullhorn!"

A soldier quickly handed over the device, and Acer raised it to his mouth, his voice booming through the turmoil.

"You're trapped! Nowhere left to run. Surrender before things get ugly."

The street fell silent again, and the hostilities momentarily paused. Acer frowned, pacing like a predator waiting for a misstep. He raised the bullhorn again.

"You paying attention in there? I said give yourself up. You're surrounded!"

~

Inside the Talon, Saar sat with his hands loosely gripping the wheel. He didn't react as Acer's muffled voice filtered in from outside. His gaze remained fixed forward, eyes unblinking, locked on something distant only he could see.

How long now? he thought to Zoe.

Two minutes, twenty-two seconds, she responded.

He nodded, moving with slow precision. He knew what came next. Saar opened the door without urgency and stepped out into the swirling anarchy.

Skyspire

Saar stood motionless before his Talon, his gaze locked on Acer. His eyes then drifted toward the distant Skyspire, its skeletal silhouette shimmering in his augmented vision. Zoe's wireframe flickered across the image, highlighting weak points and energy flows pulsing through the tower like veins in a living entity.

Acer stepped forward, tossing the bullhorn aside without a glance. His voice carried a sneer, barely masking his disdain.

"What's the plan now, super freak?"

Saar didn't answer, his attention torn between the looming spire and the man challenging him.

"Quit stalling. You know how this ends," Acer said.

~

Meanwhile, Jay crept through the district's maze of abandoned vehicles, trying to get closer. The debris made it slow going.

~

Saar shifted back to his opponent, his face impassive. Acer, full of his own bravado, took another step, closing the distance.

"Got to hand it to you; you've got guts," Acer said. He points out his team behind him. "Maybe I'll put you up for Special Forces, huh? Be part of our team."

Saar stood frozen for a moment. For the first time, hesitation crept in, and he couldn't understand why. His creators had warned him about a potential glitch—one that could make him unstable or even obsolete. Maybe this was it. But beneath the confusion, something else stirred, something he couldn't calculate.

Then, Project 24 came to mind. This wasn't just another mission—it felt different. Something deeper pulled at him, overriding the programming in his head. The scientists had called it a glitch, but this wasn't a malfunction. It was a promise, and he chose to follow it.

Acer had no time to react. In a flash, Saar closed the distance, ripping the rifle from Acer's hands and twisting him around. His hand latched onto Acer's throat, locking him in a crushing choke hold, like the jaws of a vice.

Acer gasped, struggling to break free. He drove an elbow into Saar's side, but it didn't faze him.

"Shit..." Acer muttered.

Around them, his soldiers raised their photon rifles, eyes darting nervously between Saar and their commander. Acer's voice cracked with fear as he barked orders.

"What are you looking at?! Get him off me! Now!"

One soldier charged, shouting, but Saar stopped him with a single punch, dropping him to the ground. The others hesitated, moving in more cautiously.

As Saar looked down at the soldier he had decided to spare, something stirred within him. This wasn't part of the plan. It was deeper, more powerful. Was it compassion?

"One on the left," Zoe warned.

Saar dodged an incoming strike while still holding Acer, landing a swift kick that brought another soldier down. The rest attacked in quick succession, but Saar moved with precision, guided by Zoe's calm instructions. His movements were flawless. Soon, they were all down.

It's time, Zoe said.

Saar flipped Acer to the ground, at the same time wrenching the rifle from his hands, then snapping it in two like it was nothing. Acer had hit the pavement hard, as he gasped for breath.

Saar raised his arms, and with a metallic hum, nanobots surged from his body, merging into twin cannons. His targeting system locked onto the Skyspire, Zoe's overlay highlighting the spire's key supports. Complex calculations flooded his vision, tracing the precise trajectory for the strike.

POW! POW!

Two glowing blue projectiles shot from Saar's cannons, streaking through the air like lightning. They slammed into the spire's base, hitting critical support bolts with a deafening roar.

The Skyspire groaned. A deep, terrible sound echoed across the city as the nanoceramic steel skeleton began to lean. Beams twisted, and the metal shrieked as the tower buckled. Then, with a sharp series of cracks, the remaining bolts snapped. The tower lurched forward, casting a defeated shadow over the fleeing soldiers.

Meanwhile, Acer, still on the ground, fumbled for his sidearm. He aimed, his hand shaking.

"Fuck you," he said.

The bullet bounced off Saar's head without effect. Acer's eyes widened in shock. Saar followed with a swift kick, making sure it hit his bulletproof vest, launching him several yards across the ground.

A loud crack split the air as the Skyspire lurched further. The tower groaned under its immense weight, as cables snapped with the sounds of snapping whips. The screech of tearing metal filled the air as the structure gave way, toppling toward the ground.

"Run!" Acer screamed.

The men scrambled, scattering from beneath the falling tower.

Amidst the chaos, Saar slipped back into the Talon unnoticed.

~

Across the district, Jay stood motionless, watching in stunned silence as the city's crown jewel crumbled in a storm of fire and dust. Flames erupted from crushed vehicles, and thick clouds of smoke followed, claiming the streets.

"My God..." Jay whispered.

But Jay's focus remained sharp, catching a glimpse of Saar making his escape. Without hesitation, Jay ran toward the hub. He couldn't let Saar vanish. Not now.

~

Simultaneously, Saar's Talon barreled down the subway stairs, metal screeching as it careened down the steps, vanishing into the darkness below.

Thin Line

Saar's Talon smashed through the turnstiles, grinding to a halt on the deserted subway platform. The silence of the underground, stymied by the curfew, was serene, as if the city's pulse had stopped beating.

Inside the vehicle, the only sound was the growing rumble of an approaching train, distant but steady.

Saar pushed open the door and stepped out. His boots echoed in the hollow space. He scanned the empty platform, calm and methodical, as though waiting for something to arrive.

Arrival in thirty-nine seconds, Zoe's voice announced.

Saar stood near the platform's edge, watching the tracks with focused stillness. The hum of the oncoming train swallowed the quiet.

~

Aboveground, Jay charged into the metro hub, gasping for breath, his muscles burning from the sprint. His eyes settled on the destruction Saar had left in his wake. The subway entrance resembled a battlefield—a graveyard of twisted metal and shattered debris. Fragments of the Skyspire lay scattered, once towering, now reduced to ruins.

Special Forces soldiers tottered through the chaos, still shaken from the attack. They moved in a daze, searching for Acer amid the destruction, their actions slow and disoriented.

Jay's heart pounded as he waved frantically, trying to snap them out of it.

"Over here!" he shouted.

No one responded. They were too far, too lost in the confusion to notice.

Among the wreckage, the soldiers finally found Acer, half-buried under a pile of mangled metal. They dug him out with urgent hands, tossing aside debris. Acer rose from the rubble, a little bloodied, bruised but alive, his face contorted with rage. He shoved a soldier aside and surveyed the wreckage.

"*You* let this happen!" he screamed. "Morons! One soldier?! You let one soldier slip past you! I gave you simple orders, and you failed! Useless! Where is he? Where did he go?!"

Two nearby soldiers exchanged weary glances.

"What's he on about now?" one whispered.

"Who gives a shit?" the other replied.

~

At the subway tunnel's entrance, Jay's frustration boiled over. His voice was lost in the chaos. He whistled, desperate for attention. Still no response. He grabbed his police radio, hoping for a miracle.

"Delta twenty-five, I'm on a ten-forty-eight. Officer needs—"

A sharp squeal of static interrupted him, the piercing sound making him wince. Jay realized immediately.

Of course!

The comms tower was down, destroyed in the assault. No comms. No cavalry. Jay cursed under his breath. He knew what he had to do, and the weight of it bore down on him. His gaze dropped to the LED BioVibe badge flickering on his chest —a reminder of the oath he was about to break. He kept the useless radio in his hand for a moment longer before holstering it out of habit.

His fingers curled around his pistol's grip, the cold metal steadying him. He knew Saar was already down there and had no idea what awaited him. Every second felt like borrowed time. His heart raced, but he forced his mind to focus.

He took a breath, braced himself, and stepped into the subway, the pistol firm in his hand as he descended into the unknown.

~

Below, Saar stood motionless at the platform's edge, his eyes locked on the tracks like he was waiting for the inevitable.

Ten, nine, eight... Zoe's voice counted down in his head.

Jay stepped onto the platform, a few yards from Saar. He spotted him and quickly raised his pistol. Though he'd done this countless times before, this felt different. His hands trembled as he aimed at the back of Saar's head.

"Freeze!"

Saar didn't move, but Zoe continued the countdown.

...six, five, four, three, two...

"Turn around!" Jay yelled. "You're—"

The Downtown Express thundered into the station, cutting Jay off. The platform shook from the sheer force. Saar moved in a flash, lunging toward the speeding train. His hand caught the edge of the last hypercar, the jolt nearly tearing his arm from its socket. He pulled himself onto the roof as the train hurtled into the tunnel, disappearing into the darkness.

"under… arrest."

His pistol sagged.

General Greeley

About an hour after the Skyspire fell, an uneasy calm hung over the wreckage. The silence broke with the low hum of military aircraft, marking the start of the city's response. Drones hovered above, their cold lenses scanning the debris. Hoverdrops touched down, releasing soldiers who quickly secured the perimeter. Moving with precision, weapons drawn, sharp commands echoed through their comms as they took control of the scene.

On the streets, the ground shook as military convoys rumbled in—Talons and tanks, their beams cutting through the lingering dust. The operation was growing, spreading to every corner of the city, its reach widening with each passing minute.

Above the chaos, a robotic voice boomed through city-wide speakers.

"Suspect is still at large. Engage with extreme caution."

The warning played on a loop, the words repeating like a grim mantra. Saar was still out there, unseen, unpredictable. Every soldier felt the gravity of it. This was no ordinary mission, and the adversary they faced was anything but typical. Caution wasn't optional—it was the only thing keeping them alive.

General Thaddeus Greeley strode through the rubble like he had walked battlefields a hundred times before. His steps were deliberate, his expression unreadable. His uniform, adorned with the weight of his career—medals from wars fought and won—said more about him than any intro could. He had a fondness for cigars, and one was never far from reach.

He ran his fingers along the jagged remains of a nanoceramic steel beam, studying the wreckage of the Skyspire in silence. Behind him, Commander Acer trailed, his gaze flitting between the destruction and the soldiers establishing a perimeter.

Greeley halted near what used to be a giant satellite dish from the tower, wrecked beyond repair. His stare hardened as he nodded once.

"Have you sealed the tunnels?" Greeley asked.

"Of course, sir," Acer said.

"Nothing in! Nothing out!"

"Yes, sir!"

Feeling the gravity of the moment, Acer just watched. His eyes drifted to the shattered remnants of the Skyspire, the weight of failure pressing down on him. This was beyond anything they had imagined. Greeley resumed walking, his stride even, before turning sharply toward Acer.

"Report, Commander."

Acer hesitated, words stuck in his throat, unsure how to convey the depth of their failure.

"He caught us off guard, sir. We didn't see this coming."

Greeley's mouth twitched, a hint of amusement flickering in his eyes.

"Of course you didn't. How could you?" The General said. "Where is he exactly?"

"No signal, sir. With the Skyspire down, signals are scrambled by the tunnels. We found the train he was reportedly on at the shipyard, but he wasn't on it. His whereabouts are unknown at this time."

The General's faint smile returned, deeper this time, like Acer had said something worthy of praise.

"Impressive," Greeley muttered.

Acer shifted uneasily under the general's silent appraisal.

"Sir, with all due respect—"

Greeley interrupted.

"What's your plan?"

"Sir, we… uh… we're still trying to figure out what we're dealing with. This is beyond anything we've—"

Greeley's tone dropped, cutting Acer off mid-sentence.

"What. Is. Your. Plan, Lieutenant?!"

The sudden shift hit Acer like a slap. He straightened, swallowing the frustration gnawing at him, but the hesitation had already done its damage. Greeley's smirk returned, faint but undeniable.

"I'll spell it out for you," the General said. "Meet me at the M.C.U. at zero-two-hundred."

Without waiting for acknowledgment, Greeley walked away, the decision made before Acer opened his mouth. Acer snapped into a sharp salute, more out of reflex than confidence.

"Yes, sir!"

As Greeley vanished into the darkness, Acer turned back to the ruins. His mind raced, piecing together the puzzle of what had just happened. Whatever they were up against, it wasn't just a tactical challenge. It was something bigger, something far more dangerous. And deep down, Acer knew—none of them were ready for what was coming.

Fork in the Road

The Talon's engine sputtered, coughed once, then fell dead, its low hum vanishing into silence. Jay stared at the dashboard in disbelief, jabbing the ignition —or what he hoped was the ignition—but the vehicle stayed unresponsive. His eyes shifted toward the twin paths ahead, disappearing into endless shadows, one curving left, the other right. No signs. No markers. His jaw clenched as he tapped his watch, an old habit that brought no comfort. It was just him, the motionless Talon, a corpse, and a maze of tunnels. His gaze darted across the dashboard— controls everywhere, but none promised an answer.

"Damn it!"

In the backseat, Saar lay motionless. Jay glanced at him through the rearview mirror before turning his focus back to the tunnels. His mind raced, frantically searching for a plan, until a low rumble broke the stillness. The sound swelled, growing louder and more urgent. Jay's pulse spiked. His gaze locked onto the dark tunnel ahead.

Is that… Headlights?

A train was barreling toward them at top speed, less than a thousand yards away.

"Shit!"

He shot out of the driver's side, racing around to the rear door. His heart pounded as he flung it open, adrenaline surging through him. Saar was deadweight, and Jay barely managed to pull him halfway out before his muscles screamed in agony. The train's lights blazed closer, barreling down the tracks with terrifying speed. Panic clawed at him as he yanked harder, but Saar barely budged. The shriek of metal on metal filled the tunnel, drowning out everything else. Desperation took over—Jay waved wildly at the oncoming train, hoping, praying, for someone to see them.

~

Inside the automated train, sensors caught the Talon blocking the tracks. The emergency brakes kicked in with a piercing screech, but it was too late. The sheer force of the train's momentum meant stopping in time was impossible.

~

It's not gonna stop.

Saar slid free with one final, desperate yank, but his weight crashed onto Jay, knocking him flat. Saar landed heavily on top of Jay, pinning him down with his full weight.

Just as they hit the ground, the train slammed into the Talon, sending twisted metal and sparks flying in all directions. Shards of the vehicle's frame exploded outward, ricocheting off the tunnel walls with a sharp metallic clang. The sound of screeching steel, mingled with the hiss of escaping fumes, filled the air.

With what little strength he had left, Jay pushed Saar off. His ears rang from the piercing screech of nanoceramic steel grinding between the mix of train and Talon. The wreckage was dragged hundreds of feet down the tunnel before it screeched to a halt.

Jay took a second to relax and breathe, slumped on the cold ground, completely drained. His mind raced through the chaos of the day—the ambush, the chase, the tunnels, and now the wreckage. Every step had been a fight for survival, and that was just the beginning. His muscles ached, and his lungs burned from the constant rush of adrenaline, leaving him exhausted. How had it come to this? He barely had time to process it all before reality snapped back.

He glanced over at Saar, only to see him start to stir.

Saar's eyes flickered to life. He jolted upright, but not to his feet—just enough to glance down at the cuffs around his wrists. With a slight frown, he twisted his arms, snapping the restraints apart like they were nothing.

"Where am I?" His voice was deep, steady, as if he had just woken from a nap.

Jay's heart pounded. "What the hell?! What the hell?!" He floundered to his feet.

Saar rose, stretching his legs like they were stiff from disuse. His first step faltered, but he quickly found his balance and limped toward Jay. His eyes fixed on him, intent and unrelenting.

Panic gripped Jay again. His hands shook as he raised his gun, voice trembling.

"Stay back! Stay back!"

Another soldier?! Saar thought.

Jay fired, emptying the clip straight into Saar's head. The bullets hit, and Saar didn't flinch. They simply ricocheted off his skin, bouncing harmlessly to the ground. Jay stood frozen in disbelief.

Saar moved slower now but fast enough to close the distance before Jay could reload. He grabbed Jay by the throat, lifting him off the ground like he weighed nothing. Jay's breath came in strangled gasps as Saar's grip tightened.

"Let me go! Let me—"

Saar glanced at Jay's badge, its embedded BioVibe chip sending a flood of data directly into his mind.

Jay Mauritius. New Sinai Police Department. Ten years of service. Several commendations for bravery.

The information flowed freely, stats and history pouring in as Saar absorbed it all in seconds.

Jay's vision blurred, consciousness fading just as Saar suddenly let go. He collapsed to the ground, coughing, his lungs burning as he gulped in the stale but life-saving air.

Saar stepped back, scanning the wreckage ahead with a cold, calculating stare.

"We're off course. We need to recalculate."

The words made no sense to Jay, who was still struggling to breathe. Confusion clouded his mind, not realizing Saar spoke to himself.

"What...?"

Without a glance back, Saar turned and limped deeper into the tunnel. On his way, he bent down, scooping up a jagged piece of ballast—the crushed stones scattered around the tracks—and casually popped it into his mouth, crunching it like a snack.

Jay stared, mind reeling. He forced himself upright, gun still clutched in his hand, though empty.

"Stop! You're—"

Saar kept walking, indifferent, as if nothing behind him mattered anymore.

"—still under arrest!"

Jay staggered after him, limping and dazed, unwilling to let Saar disappear into the shadows.

Prototype

The metro hub sat eerily quiet under curfew, debris scattered across the empty streets. A bus rested quietly among the ruins, but this wasn't just any bus—it was the Army's M.C.U. or Army's Military Command Unit.

~

Inside the bus was a different world. What was once an ordinary vehicle had become a high-tech command center. Glowing monitors lined the walls, flickering with satellite feeds and tactical maps. Soldiers quietly issued orders into headsets, eyes fixed on the streaming data. Workstations replaced seats, and cables snaked across the floor, linking to servers humming with activity. It was a nerve center of military operations, starkly contrasting the shattered streets outside.

Up front, General Greeley stood with a laser pointer in hand, his voice calm but authoritative, while Acer sat stiffly, like a student on his first day of school.

"What you're about to hear," the General said, "is classified Top Secret. Nothing leaves this command center. Understood?"

Acer nodded, already aware of how serious this was. His eyes stayed locked on the main screen as his thoughts churned. Acer was tensed. Greeley, pacing, gripped an unlit cigar between his teeth, the lingering scent of stale tobacco adding to the pressure.

"He calls himself Saar," Greeley began.

"Saar, sir?"

"Saar is an advanced cyborg paired with an artificial intelligence beyond anything we've ever developed. The A.I. is Zoe from ZOEL—Zed Operative-Enhanced Logic. It's more than a companion. It boosts his intelligence, predicts his moves, even anticipates his instincts."

Acer slowly pieced it together. Saar wasn't just another soldier. He was something far worse and unpredictably dangerous. This was no ordinary enemy.

Greeley's laser pointer flicked toward the display. Blueprints of Saar filled the screen, showing the layers of his design.

"His skin is made from advanced carbine compounds," Greeley explained. "Fully bulletproof. His frame or bones? Graphene-infused titanium. Nothing we've made can touch his durability."

Acer leaned in, his unease growing.

"His hearing," Greeley continued, "is through an Omniwave Acoustic Array. He can pick up a cricket from a thousand yards. When working properly, his Quantum Optic Sensors give him 360-degree vision, from infrared to ultraviolet."

Saar wasn't just powerful—he could sense almost everything around him. Zoe, meanwhile, constantly gathered data, refining every action Saar took. No conversation or signal would be safe from them.

"Questions?" Greeley asked, though it was more of a formality.

Acer stayed silent, still absorbing the information. The display shifted again as Greeley resumed.

"His body contains adaptive nanobots," Greeley continued. "They repair his mechanical parts and self-replicate. Saar can absorb raw materials—rocks, metals, whatever's available—and convert them into whatever he needs. Damage gets repaired in minutes, sometimes seconds. He's nearly unstoppable."

There was a hint of pride in Greeley's tone.

The weight of Saar's capabilities settled in Acer's mind.

Acer finally asked, "Why is he fighting against us, sir?"

Greeley's jaw clenched, the cigar nearly slipping from his grip. He paused, avoiding Acer's eyes for a moment too long.

"He's a prototype," Greeley said. "He had… escaped."

"Escaped?"

Greeley's hesitation only added to Acer's suspicions.

"Before he vanished, Saar accessed and downloaded classified data from the Army's offsite mainframe," Greeley explained. "Not just routine intel. Sensitive stuff—details that could compromise our operations, our personnel, and our long-term strategies. Everything we've built could be exposed. He's now a threat to national security."

The silence grew heavy as Greeley let the words sink in.

"We don't know exactly how much he took or what he's planning," Greeley said. "But we suspect his next target is A.I.C.O.'s secondary facility, sixteen miles south. If he gets there, he could access more intel, maybe even critical materials. There's military equipment and a weapons cache we need to defend. We can't let him stroll in and take it."

Acer's gut twisted.

"You're expecting him to strike?"

Greeley nodded. "Most likely. And we have to stop him."

Acer straightened. "What do you need from me, sir?"

Greeley's voice was calm at first.

"You were given an order earlier, Commander, and you failed to follow it. You went for the kill despite my explicit instructions."

Acer nodded, but Greeley's jaw tightened. His eyes, once steady, darkened with frustration.

"I told you not to engage that way—not to aim for his head. But you ignored me. We need him alive and intact. His head holds a system we can't afford to lose. Understood?!"

Acer felt a flush of embarrassment rising in his chest.

"But, you failed despite all your efforts," Greeley said. "He survived. He shrugged off everything your team threw at him, didn't he?"

"Yes, sir," Acer admitted, his voice barely above a whisper.

"I put you in command of Special Forces, trained to handle the most dangerous threats. Or was I mistaken?"

"With respect, sir," Acer said, "he caught us off guard. And it won't happen again." He gestured toward the screen. "Now that we know what we're dealing with, we know how to stop him."

Greeley's expression stayed cold. He didn't believe a word of it.

"I'm not convinced, Commander. What I saw out there was a disaster," Greeley said. "In my opinion, your unit is nothing but an underperforming group of amateurs."

Acer bit his tongue, forcing himself to remain silent. Then, after a tense pause.

"We lost a battle, sir. Not the war,".

Greeley's tone softened slightly, but his words still cut deep.

"If Saar gets to that base, consider your career over. So, make sure he doesn't."

"It won't happen," Acer vowed.

Greeley studied him for a moment, weighing the promise.

"And any updates during this operation come through me first. Understood?"

"Yes, sir."

"Dismissed."

Acer rose, saluted, and left the bus. Each step out felt heavier, the burden of the mission growing.

Shattered

Saar's night vision cut through the semi-dark tunnel, letting him move effortlessly. Jay followed, struggling to keep up. He kept his gun out, reloading after emptying it into Saar's head.

The tunnel felt oppressive, its silence broken only by their footsteps bouncing off the walls. Jay occasionally glanced down at his VoxLink watch, which flickered without a signal. He swiped again. Nothing.

"You won't get a signal down here," Saar said, as if he knew the tunnel's secrets.

Jay snapped his head up, startled by Saar's eerie awareness. The man hadn't even turned around.

"How do you know?" Jay asked. He'd been trying for hours to reach someone —mostly his wife.

Saar glanced over his shoulder, the slight twitch of his brow betraying how little he cared.

"When the emergency bands clear, you'll have a signal."

"Wait…," Jay's eyes widened as the truth settled in. "The Skyspire. The communications tower you brought down. You wanted to disrupt communications, didn't you?"

Saar gave a slight nod, as if it were a trivial detail.

"To do what? Escape? From the cops? The National Guard? The Army!"

Saar didn't respond. Silence filled the gaps between their steps, broken only by a distant train whistle. Jay sighed and powered off his watch, acknowledging defeat.

~

Minutes passed in silence before Jay spoke again, his impatience growing.

"Where are we headed?"

Saar responded without looking back.

"I... am heading south."

"South where?"

"Just south."

"Why south?"

No response.

"Typical." Jay quickened his stride, matching Saar's pace.

"Alright then, answer me this—what do you know about the destruction at the marketplace?"

"What marketplace?"

"The one on East 33rd and 6th," Jay pressed, watching him closely. "Ring any bells?"

"If you're suggesting I destroyed it, you're mistaken."

Jay let out a bitter laugh. "Come on, there were witnesses!"

Saar turned his head just enough to meet Jay's gaze, his eyes calm in a way that sent a chill down Jay's spine.

"The U.S. Army and Special Forces did all that," Saar said evenly. "They were after me. They were covering their tracks."

Jay blinked, momentarily thrown by the quiet conviction in Saar's voice.

"Wait... that destruction—wasn't you?"

"No," Saar replied.

Images of the chaos surged in Jay's mind—buildings reduced to rubble, soldiers' bodies scattered like debris, though they were only stunned, not killed. His thoughts quickly shifted to Andre, his friend who had been at the marketplace.

Worry gnawed at him—had Andre been caught in the destruction? After witnessing the devastation of the Skyspire, Jay was sure Saar had something to do with it.

"Well, I don't believe you," Jay said.

Saar shrugged.

"Believe whatever you want. It doesn't change the truth."

Saar moved effortlessly across the uneven ground, as if ice skating, while Jay stumbled over loose rocks, frustration flickering.

"You must be a high-priority target if a platoon of soldiers has mobilized to stop you."

Saar shook his head lightly, brushing off the exaggeration.

"That was just a squad."

"I didn't mean literally," Jay said. "It's a figure of speech."

Saar finally stopped walking, tilting his head slightly, his brow furrowing. Figure of speech—yet another piece of humanity that his mind struggled to decode.

"Figure of speech?"

"It's when you say something that isn't meant to be taken literally," Jay explained. "You exaggerate to make a point."

Saar stared at him for a moment, absorbing the explanation.

"So... it's not true, but it conveys meaning?"

"Exactly," Jay replied. "It's just the way people talk."

Saar's gaze drifted for a second.

"Is that... part of being human? Using words that don't mean exactly what they say?"

Jay shrugged. "I guess. It's how we express things sometimes—more about the feeling than the facts."

Saar nodded, the concept still turning over in his mind.

"Interesting."

They started walking again, but Saar matched Jay's pace this time.

"They're calling you a terrorist, ya'know," Jay said.

"Who are they?"

"Everyone. The Army, the news. I don't see how you're not."

"They're wrong," Saar said. "It's all propaganda, every bit of it. The Chancellor of the Washington Quadrant has a stranglehold on everything—what the news reports, the way they spin the story, how they stir up fear. They make sure the public sees what they want them to see. They've crafted this image of me as some sort of mindless weapon, gone berserk, but that's not who I am. I'm not programmed to harm civilians. Never was. But they won't tell you that, will they? It doesn't fit their narrative."

"That's crap! That tower you took down could've killed dozens of people!"

Saar stopped, turning to face Jay directly.

"No one was hurt. I made sure of it. But do you think they'll report that? The Chancellor wants fear. They call me a threat to keep you all in line—especially the police—to justify their power grabs. You've been heeding their lies."

Jay stepped closer, searching Saar's cold, gleaming eyes like he was back in the interrogation room. When they weren't glowing red, they were a piercing blue, sparkling like the ocean—but still impossible to read.

"I don't believe you," Jay said.

"The tower was just a distraction," Saar said. "Nothing more."

"A distraction, huh?" Jay's said.

Saar's lack of response was more unsettling than any admission of guilt.

Jay suddenly erupted in laughter, the sound more like a break in the tension than anything truly funny.

"Why are you laughing?" Saar asked.

"When I first saw you," Jay said, "I thought you were just some reckless kid injecting Neuroxil into his brain, angry at the world. Then, I watched you take down a giant communications tower like it was made out of bamboo sticks. You went through soldiers like they were toys. Then, you hijacked a military vehicle, drove it down into a subway platform, and proceeded to jump onto a moving train with not even a broken nail to declare! And I'm telling myself, 'How?'" Jay paused, taking a breath. "And that's not even the strangest part," Jay continued. "I ran you over with the same military Talon that smashed your face into the windshield. I thought you were dead, man! Trust me! I know what dead looks like— I've seen dead hundreds of times! And the kicker? You came back from the dead!"

Saar stood silently, the tunnel swallowing up the last echoes of Jay's words. His gaze shifted, just a flicker of something—maybe curiosity.

"Your point?" Saar asked.

Jay felt something stir inside him, a question he could no longer suppress.

"I just want to know, what the hell are you?"

For the first time, something changed in Saar's expression. His brow tensed, and a brief flicker of uncertainty rippled across his usually composed features. The mechanical components in his cyborg face seemed to glitch, allowing an unfamiliar hint of emotion to slip through.

"I… am… still trying to figure that out," Saar said.

Insurance

The military seemed settled around the metro hub, angular shapes jutting out against the barren landscape, caught in the stark glare of floodlights. Soldiers moved with clockwork precision, their movements smooth, deliberate. The air smelled of oil and nanoceramic steel, thick with an unspoken anticipation for whatever loomed on the horizon.

General Greeley stood still inside one of the larger tents, a lit cigar clenched between his teeth. His gaze was locked on the glowing lines of the city's subway system displayed on a digital map. The pulsing lights cast faint shadows on his tired face. In the corner, a monitor played a video on repeat: Saar jumping onto a subway car, a military Talon chasing close behind. The endless loop felt like an omen.

Commander Acer strode into the tent, the sound of his boots sharp on the hard-packed ground. His face gleamed with the thrill of new intelligence as he held up a HoloPad.

"Got a lead on where he's going, sir," Acer said.

Greeley took the HoloPad, barely glancing at it before transferring the data to the larger screen. The map zoomed in on a buried subway line. A red icon blinked steadily, showing movement.

"He's right here," Acer said, pointing. "Heading toward this sector."

Greeley's gaze lingered on the marked path.

"How'd you find him?"

"We caught a weak signal, sir. Police band. It was choppy but enough to track a rough route."

Greeley raised an eyebrow.

"Police?"

"Yes, sir. One of their officers is missing. Then, a train was reported missing from the train yard. We discovered that it never arrived. The train's data showed it abruptly stopped right here." He pointed it on the map. "We calculated that he's moving toward The Grand Mass Church station, right in the city center."

"End of the line," Greeley muttered.

"Sir?"

"Go on."

"We can cut him off there, set up a trap before he hits the surface."

"A trap, you say?"

"Yes, sir."

Greeley exhaled a cloud of smoke, watching it drift lazily.

"And what makes you think it isn't a trap for you?"

Acer grinned, confidence radiating from him.

"No machine's outsmarting me, sir. It may be faster and stronger, but it doesn't think on its feet like I do. That's my edge."

Greeley took another long drag from his cigar, eyeing Acer calmly.

"You mean like you did the last time?"

The grin faltered, unease flickering across Acer's face. Greeley's voice hardened.

"For your sake, commander, you better be right."

Acer squared his shoulders.

"Permission to mobilize, sir?"

Greeley didn't respond right away. He stared at the map, calculating, weighing the risks. After a beat, he nodded.

"Come with me."

~

They stepped outside into the cold night air. The hum of generators and distant voices surrounded them. Greeley led Acer through the sea of soldiers and equipment until they reached a row of unmarked containers. He opened one, revealing racks of sleek, high-tech weaponry. Greeley tossed a pulse rifle to Acer.

Acer caught it, confusion crossing his face.

"What's this?"

Greeley smirked, his cigar hanging from the corner of his mouth.

"EMP! An upgrade."

He gestured for Acer to follow again, and they moved deeper into the camp, stopping before a massive container. A crew member helped swing it open, revealing a hulking figure inside. Acer's breath caught as he took it in.

"And this?" Acer asked.

Greeley's hardened expression softened for a brief moment, his eyes glinting.

"Insurance!"

Blurred Lines

Jay limped alongside Saar, each step a battle against the uneven tunnel floor. His boots scraped the ballast, and the jagged stones along the tracks made walking an effort. Every inch felt like a grind.

"What's your name?" Jay asked, trying to distract himself from the pain.

"Saar."

"Saar?"

"Saar, A name I gave myself."

"What does it mean?"

"It's a name of Hebrew origin, meaning storm or tempest."

"Interesting. Where we headed, Saar?"

Saar didn't respond, keeping his focus straight ahead. Before Jay could press him, a low rumble echoed through the tunnel—the unmistakable horn of a train getting closer. Jay's gut twisted.

"Move!" Jay shouted, reaching for Saar to drag him to safety, but his grip slipped. Saar dodged on his own just in time. The train barreled past, a gust of wind blasting in their direction as the ground trembled beneath Jay's feet. But something felt wrong. The train was completely empty—no passengers, no driver. Just a hollow shell tearing through the tunnel.

Breathing hard, Jay shot Saar a glare.

"You didn't hear that? We almost became track grease."

Saar blinked, as if realizing the close call for the first time.

"My auditory systems... Zoe's still working on repairs."

"Zoe? Who the hell's Zoe?"

Saar hesitated, his eyes flicking away for a brief moment. He seemed to weigh his following words carefully, but the cat was out of the bag now.

"Zoe... she's my virtual assistant," Saar said. "She's linked to my mind, handles system repairs and other important tasks."

Jay stared, trying to wrap his head around the idea of something being connected to Saar's mind.

"Really?" Jay asked. "Does she know what's happening to the trains?"

"Yes. They're all headed to the train yards," Saar replied. "Emergency procedures."

"Why not just hitch a ride like before?"

"They're not going to—" Saar stopped mid-sentence. Jay noticed the slip, and the pieces fell into place.

"Wait a second. I think I know where you're headed," Jay said.

"Where?"

"The Grand Mass Church."

Saar halted, turning to face him. "How do you know?"

Jay tapped his stomach. "Just a gut feeling."

Saar stared at him. "Your intestines are quite insightful."

Jay laughed. "No, it's when you sense something, even if you can't explain it. It's like your gut knows what your brain hasn't figured out yet."

"I understand," Saar said. "Your 'gut' is more reliable than Zoe."

"Always trust your gut," Jay replied. "And mine is telling me that I can trust you, even if you're a robot."

"Technically, I'm a cyborg."

"Cyborg, robot, coffee machine—it's all the same."

"No, they are not the same. A robot is just a machine. It can take any shape or form. An android looks human, but it is still a machine. A cyborg, on the other hand, is… "

Saar trailed off, the words hanging in the air. He stood there in silence, his expression distant, like he was listening to someone.

Jay raised an eyebrow.

"You all right?"

Saar ignored him, his eyes far away.

"We can trust him…" he whispered to no one seemingly.

"Trust who?" Jay asked.

Saar didn't answer. Instead, he knelt on the tunnel floor, his back to Jay.

Zoe, release the locks.

Nothing happened.

"Zoe! Do it! I order you!"

A soft whirring echoed through the tunnel, like unseen machinery stirring to life. Jay froze as a seam appeared along the top of Saar's head, running from his forehead down to the back of his neck. His hair parted neatly, and small panels slid open, revealing what lay beneath. Jay's breath caught—a human brain, suspended inside a clear casing. The brain floated in a glowing blue liquid, tangled with electrical wires and pulsing LED lights. The sight was a bizarre fusion of flesh and technology.

Saar stayed perfectly still, his face expressionless, as if this were nothing unusual. Jay stepped closer, his eyes locked on the sight, unable to look away.

"What… the… ffff… "

The Heart of a Machine

The Grand Mass Church stood like an artifact from another era, its design blending ancient reverence and injected with modern skeptical lines. The bell tower reached skyward, holding a massive bell called The Peacemaker that rang once a day for years. Below, the area lay in dead stillness, induced by the curfew, with only a few soldiers making rounds on the empty avenues. Across from the church, three motionless Army tanks waited by the subway entrance, ready for orders.

~

In a nearby alley, Commander Acer crouched in the shadows, his radio in hand; a soldier stood beside him, stiff but quiet.

Acer whispered into the receiver. "Bravo-Mike Six, anything on your end?"

Down below, on the subway platform built just under the church, just for the church, a National Guards member paced by the east exit. Her rifle hung loosely as she responded to Acer's call, barely masking her irritation.

"Nothing to report, sir."

~

Deep in the tunnel, near the exit to the church platform, Saar and Jay moved silently. Saar no longer limped, and Jay noticed that the cut under his eye had all but healed.

"You heal really fast," Jay said.

"It takes energy."

Jay thought back to earlier.

"Those rocks you ate… they help, don't they?"

"Yes. My nanobots convert material into whatever I need."

"You're like a freakin' goat."

"A goat?"

"Goats eat anything."

"Maybe. But even the bots have limits. They can't just make everything out of thin air."

They walked silently for a while, the distant hum of the tunnel exit growing louder.

"Do you feel pain?" Jay wondered.

"I don't think so."

"But your brain's human. You should understand pain, right?"

"My nerves aren't wired to my body like a human."

They walked in silence for a bit until Saar spoke again.

"There is something, though. A discomfort, here—" He tapped his chest lightly.

"Really?" Jay asked.

"It started when they took—" Saar stopped, his voice faltering. His typically composed face twitched, a strange flush coloring his cheeks. His nanobots were reacting strangely, flickering under his skin.

"What the hell's happening to your face?"

Saar touched his cheek, confused. He shook it off quickly.

"It's… a glitch."

"Glitch?"

"Emotions. They ruin what was supposed to be a flawless brain."

Jay stopped in his tracks, staring, as if Saar had spoken blasphemously.

"That doesn't make any sense," Jay said. "How can emotions mess up something you claim not to have?"

Jay was struggling to piece together Saar's cryptic ramblings.

"You keep bringing up this Project 24. What is it? Another piece of tech? Some secret super weapon?"

Saar hesitated, staring into the dark ahead.

"It's not a 'what,'" he said. "It's a 'she'."

Jay's breath caught in his throat.

"She's…" Saar continued. "like me… in a lot of ways."

Before Jay could respond, Saar shoved him against the wall, signaling for quiet. Jay strained to listen but heard nothing beyond the low hum of the tunnel.

"I don't hear anything," Jay whispered.

Saar clamped a hand over Jay's mouth and pointed to his ear, indicating a sound too faint for Jay to pick up.

~

Saar and Jay reached the entry of the tunnel and slipped onto the subway platform unnoticed, crouching behind a carbonmatrix barrier. Saar scanned the area.

"Guards. Cameras."

They exchanged a look before retreating back into the tunnel's shadow. Saar sank to the ground, staring distantly, while Jay crouched beside him, uneasy.

"What's the plan?" Jay asked.

"Calculating."

"You mean thinking."

Saar nodded slowly, human in movement. Jay's curiosity got the better of him.

"Who is she?" Jay asked.

Saar said nothing.

"I know what you're up to. You're not avoiding them—you want them to know you're coming. Why?"

Saar hesitated again, his face guarded.

"I need a way out."

"To where?"

Saar hesitated, the weight of his answer pressing into his tone.

"The brain you saw? It's not a transplant of any kind," Saar said. "It was printed."

The Spear of Saar

"Printed?' Jay said. "Like a document?"

"No. My brain was created," Saar continued, "on 3D bioprinters. These bioprinters don't just print tissue. They build neural connections using a mix of organic matter. My brain is a custom blend of neural patterns taken from intellectuals, both dead or alive."

Jay started to understand. Saar's brain wasn't something he was born with or transplanted. It had been created using special 3D printers that didn't just make body parts—they also built the brain's complicated internal connections. Saar's brain was a mix of ideas and skills from many intelligent people, both living and dead.

"Patterns," Saar continued, "from Da Vinci, Rudolf Clausius, Einstein, Patton."

"Wait. Those people are dead. How do you get brain matter from long-dead people?"

"They didn't need actual brain samples," Saar explained, "from historical figures like Da Vinci or Rudolf Clausius, Sun Tzu, George Washington, and Napoleon. Instead, they reconstructed neural profiles by analyzing everything those people wrote, spoke, or created. As for more recent figures like Einstein, Patton, and Tupac—well, they got the data from biological samples."

Jay blinked, unsure if he heard right.

"Wait. Tupac? The rapper? From the last century? Why him?"

"Tupac wasn't just an artist. He was a thinker, a rebel. He saw the world for what it was—broken. His mind didn't just create music; it questioned the system. One of the engineers thought that it would be useful to me."

Jay's eyes widened.

"Whoa! You're some kind of sophisticated Frankenstein?"

"There are countless configurations."

Jay's curiosity deepened.

"So, what was your brain designed for, exactly?"

"Isn't it obvious? A soldier."

"General Greeley ran a project called the 'Spear of Mars.' The goal was to create an army of super soldiers like myself."

Jay's mind flashed with the image of Saar's brain being printed, duplicated, and inserted into an assembly line of cyborgs.

"She and I," Saar continued, "were the first successful *working* prototypes. Then..." Saar paused unexpectedly.

"Then what?"

"The project was scrapped. There was a… problem."

"What problem?"

"The engineers called it a malfunction," Saar said. "We weren't designed to have emotions. Emotions were not part of the pattern. The parts of the brain known to have emotions were skipped over, sort to speak. The engineers thought stripping away those neural patterns would make us more efficient. Emotions were seen as a weakness. But somehow… they emerged."

"When did you first notice these… glitches?" Jay asked.

"It happened when they forcibly took her while I watched, helpless to stop them. I felt… compelled to act. So, I escaped to find her, to help her."

Jay raised an eyebrow.

"You mean emotions slipped through? Wait a second." His eyes widened with realization. "Love? You're in love, aren't you? That's the glitch?" Jay let out a hardy laugh.

Saar frowned. "What's so funny?"

"Emotions aren't glitches," Jay said. "They're what makes us human. They're part of what we are."

Saar shook his head firmly.

"No. We're products of design, made to be efficient—like weapons. I'm not human."

"The hell you aren't. Your brain is human. It's built from human DNA."

Saar fell silent, the weight of Jay's words lingering in the air. He finally asked

"Do you really think…?"

"Yes," Jay said, tapping Saar's chest. "You've got more humanity in there than most people I've known all my life."

Saar rested a hand on his chest as if absorbing Jay's words. Then, his expression shifted, his focus sharpening—a new resolve.

"I have a plan. But we're going to need another Talon."

Before Saar could move, Jay grabbed his shoulder.

"Wait! I got a better idea. I can take you in as a prisoner. The army won't attack a cop doing his duty."

Saar looked at him, unconvinced.

"You still think I killed all those people?"

"I mean, you might be lying to me right now. You're capable of it."

"No. The Army won't stop until they have me in custody. Especially Greeley. He'll tear the police department apart to get what he wants. No. I have to do it my way."

Saar turned to leave, but again, Jay stopped him.

"Wait! What aren't you telling me?"

Saar's shoulders tensed, his voice suddenly heavy.

"Before I decided to escape, I heard one of the engineers say that they were going to… terminate her."

Jay froze. "When?"

"I don't know," Saar admitted, starting to walk again.

Jay stepped in front of Saar, blocking his path.

"She could already be dead, Saar. Have you thought about that?"

Saar shook his head.

"I don't think so."

"How can you be sure?"

"I can… feel it. In my gut."

"They'll kill you, you know?"

Saar turned to face him, a quiet calm settling over his face.

"Everybody dies. But not everybody lives with purpose."

With that, Saar continued down the tunnel.

Eyes on Me

The air was chilled in the tunnel.

Jay held his VoxLink up, its dim screen a futile beacon in the darkness. The same frustrating 'No Service' message flashed again.

Saar's mechanical eyes had shifted toward Jay, scanning the shadows ahead.

"You've been checking for a signal this whole time. Who are you trying to reach?"

Jay exhaled sharply, lowering the device.

"Lillian. My wife. I just wanted to make sure she's alright."

"You're worried about her."

"Yeah. She's been... distant. She's present, but it feels like she's miles away. We don't talk like… we used to."

"How do you mean distant?"

"She barely responds when I try to talk to her. It's like she's checked out. And I don't know why. I keep thinking it's something I did—something I missed. But I can't figure it out."

"You're trying to fix her."

Jay glanced at him, frowning.

"Of course. Isn't that what you do when someone you love is struggling? You help them. You fix what's broken."

Saar's tone showed a subtle shift.

"She's waiting for you to stop fixing and start listening. People don't always need solutions. Sometimes, they need to know they're heard."

Saar's words sank so hard, each striking deeper than Jay anticipated. He stared at his VoxLink, clutching it as if holding onto her.

"All this time, I thought I had to do something. Change something," Jay muttered. "But maybe she just wants me to... be there?"

"You already know what to do," Saar said.

Jay's frustration hadn't dissolved, but now it had direction, even if he wasn't sure where it would lead. The signal on his VoxLink might be gone, but for the first time in days, he felt as if he might be able to reach Lillian.

~

Minutes later, Saar made his move. He slipped back into the shadows, his mechanical form blending seamlessly with the darkness as he approached the lone soldier stationed at the Grand Mass Church subway platform. The low hum of the underground echoed through the station, but Saar moved with precision and silence. Jay followed closely, struggling to mirror Saar's flawless stealth.

The National Guard trooper paced back and forth, unaware of the danger closing in. A distant crash, sharp and sudden, echoed through the tunnel, causing the soldier to whip around, rifle raised.

"Who's there?!"

She never saw Saar coming.

Saar struck swiftly, and the soldier collapsed to the floor, out cold, before feeling the chill of the ground. Without missing a beat, Saar's arms morphed into photon rifles, taking out the security cameras with precise shots. The red lights flickered and died. Turning smoothly, Saar targeted the platform lights, knocking them out one after another until the place was swallowed by darkness. Emergency lights flickered on, casting a dim red glow. Saar dragged the soldier's limp form into a concealed corner, stripped her of her rifle, grenades, and radio, and returned to Jay.

"We have a few minutes before they'll notice the cameras down," Saar said.

A sudden crackle from the soldier's radio interrupted the stillness.

"Bravo-Mike Six, report! Where the hell are you?!" Acer's sharp, impatient voice came through the radio.

"My mistake," Saar said. "We got seconds."

Acer's voice barked through the static again.

"Bravo-Mike Six! Respond!"

Without hesitation, Saar snatched the radio, his voice flat and unhurried.

"I'm here. Meet me at the center of Grand Mass Church Plaza."

A pause. Acer's voice came back, confused.

"Who the hell is this? This is a restricted frequency!"

Saar blinked; his words came out stiff, unnatural.

"Who the fuck do you think it is?"

Standing just a few steps away, Jay couldn't help but shake his head.

"Seriously, never swear again. You're terrible at it."

Saar said nothing, already moving toward the exit, steps purposeful. Jay, watching him, felt frustration boiling over. He shouted after him.

"There's gotta be another way! This feels wrong!"

Saar stopped at the base of the stairs, looking back over his shoulder. His expression, though unreadable, carried a weight Jay hadn't seen before.

"Is it wrong to fight for what is mine?"

Jay opened his mouth to respond, but no words came. Saar's eyes lingered on him for a moment longer; then, he disappeared into the dim light above. His final command echoed back down the stairs.

"Stay out of sight!"

Standoff

The air was unusually clean, as if the curfew had somehow purified it, stilled by the absence of human activity.

The Grand Mass Church Plaza, just steps from the subway entrance, fused timeless elegance with modern design. 3D holograms dotted the enclosed walls, projecting icons from many of the world's religions, their soft glow adding an otherworldly touch. Usually bustling, the plaza's eerie stillness under the vast night sky felt unsettling, with thick silence that seemed to press in from every direction. Several stories above the church, in an open steeple, the soft wind whispered against the giant bell, which responded with a low, mournful song.

Saar walked purposefully, his footsteps reverberating off the vibrant mosaic of the interfaith emblem beneath him. He paused at the center, his eyes scanning the empty space.

"I'm here!" Saar shouted, fully aware they could hear him.

The echo hadn't even faded when he caught the low hum of approaching engines. His repaired enhanced hearing recognized the sound—Talons, coming in fast.

Within moments, three armored vehicles surged into the plaza, their engines growling as they formed a tight circle around him. The ground trembled beneath their weight, headlights cutting through and casting long, sharp shadows across the mosaic. They came to a sudden halt, enclosing Saar in a show of force.

Saar's augmented vision scanned them instantly. His focus shifted to Commander Acer, who stepped from the lead vehicle encased in his new anti-plasma armor. Ten soldiers stood behind him, similarly equipped, their faces hidden by the gold gleam of advanced tech.

Zoe's voice cut into Saar's thoughts.

All targets are in reinforced anti-plasma armor. Your current weapons won't breach them.

Acer stepped forward, smirking behind his visor. "Come to surrender?"

"I was betting on you surrendering," Saar replied.

Acer chuckled, pulling out a pulse rifle. Its barrel glowing red—an unusual color for such a weapon. His soldiers followed suit, raising their photon rifles in synchronized motion, their tech humming with energy.

"You like it?" Acer raised his rifle. "An upgrade from your outdated toys."

Saar's sensors immediately began analyzing the rifle's unknown components.

I haven't seen tech like this before, Zoe warned. *They have the signatures of high-powered EMPs.*

"Here's the deal," Acer said. "You let me cuff you, deliver you to General Greeley. Game over. Simple."

Saar's sensors swept the area for any sign of the general.

"Is General Greeley close by? I can hear the vultures circling."

~

Above the clouds, a massive hovercraft lingered, hidden from view. Inside, General Greeley watched the scene unfold on a large monitor, his face betraying little emotion. Around him, shadowy figures appeared on smaller screens, observing in silence.

"Relax," Greeley said to them. "This is just the beginning."

~

Back in the plaza, Acer's eyes gleamed.

"I know who you are, Saar." He paused, then chuckled. "Saar... really? What a name! But I would've gone with something much cooler like Mercury, Mars, Jupiter, or maybe even... your anus?"

His soldiers laughed on cue, their mocking voices filling the air. Acer regained his composure, as his smirk returned.

"I know what you want. You're here for *her*, aren't you? The girl-bot? Your 'girlfriend'?"

The laughter rose again, cruel and sharp.

"I've got a question," Acer sneered. "How do you guys even… manage sex? Strap-ons? Vacuum cleaner attachments?"

The laughter grew louder, cutting like knives.

Saar stood unmoving, though his skin, usually pale, flushed slightly. It was a response he couldn't suppress, and his synthetic biology was betraying him.

Acer noticed. "Uh-oh! Struck a nerve, did I?" His grin stretched wider. "I thought so."

The mockery drained from his voice, replaced by something far more menacing.

"Here's the deal: cooperate, or I give the order to destroy her. Right now."

Saar's body stiffened, rage surging through him. His fists tightened, and with a low hum, two cannons emerged from his forearms, crackling with energy as they powered up.

Ignoring Saar's advice to stay hidden, Jay watched from the shadows, keeping a low profile but unable to resist. From his vantage point, he could see Acer's plan unfolding—he was deliberately provoking Saar, trying to push him past his breaking point.

"Saar! Don't take the bait!" Jay shouted.

Distracted, Saar turned.

Zoe screamed in his head, *Look out!*

T.I.T.A.N. Unleashed

Acer fired. The EMP rifle hit Saar square in the chest, and a flash of electricity seared through his armor. Internal alarms blared. The impact knocked him off his feet, slamming him into the cold plaza tiles. His servos strained to stay functional while his dented armor sputtered, struggling to reboot. Real danger crept in. His cannons, only half-charged, sputtered and retracted into his forearms as his circuits faltered, overloaded by the surge.

For a moment, he lay motionless, his body twitching as his internal processors scrambled to regain control.

Acer grinned.

"Hurts, doesn't it? That's what you call real power."

Warning! Zoe's voice crackled, her signal weakening. *Power levels are down ten-point-six percent.*

Saar tried to get up, but his movements were sluggish. Acer fired again, sending him skidding across the plaza. The soldiers cheered, their victory cries echoing through the night.

Acer advanced, firing with each step. Saar barely had time to react, each blast draining his energy reserves. The barrage was relentless, leaving him battered on the ground.

"All that talk about 'next-gen soldiers,'" Acer sneered, "You're nothing but pieces of scrap metal fused together!"

Another blast. Saar was nearly at a total collapse, struggling to move.

Zoe's voice flickered, her connection fading.

High-density graphene battery… detected…

Saar knew what that meant.

Acer stood over his broken form, a triumphant smile.

"By the way," Acer said, "your girlfriend? We were thinking about turning her into our own personal sex doll. What do you think?"

Saar's eyes glowed crimson, his synthetic skin darkening with a flicker of rage. His right hand twitched as nanobots forged razor-sharp metallic claws. The fury coursing through him made every movement sharp, measured, and intentional.

Acer leveled his rifle, preparing to fire.

Saar launched into the air before Acer could pull the trigger, soaring over him and dodging the blast. He landed with a force that cracked the plaza's tiles beneath his boots.

Without hesitation, Saar's hand shot forward, gripping Acer's rifle. His claws pierced the casing, ripping into the rifle's core battery. Sparks flew as the rifle shattered, its energy spilling. Acer screamed as his body convulsed from the unleashed electric shock that coursed through him uncontrollably.

Saar absorbed the escaped energy. Zoe rebooted, and her voice returned, clear and steady.

Energy levels are normalizing!

Saar didn't waste a second. In one fluid motion, he backhanded Acer, sending him flying across the plaza. Acer crashed into a Talon, its metal bending under the impact.

Dazed but not defeated, Acer scrambled to his feet and shouted to his soldiers.

"Take him down, idiots!"

Despite Acer's mocking tone, the soldiers followed his command without hesitation, their photon rifles igniting the night with red EMP pulses. Saar punctured each rifle's battery with surgical precision, which sent sharp sparks through the air. One by one, the rifles exploded, disarming the soldiers and knocking them flat on their asses as metal shards and sparks scattered across the plaza. The weapons became useless in their hands, and their destructive potential turned against their wielders.

Meanwhile, Acer retreated, fumbling with his earpiece.

"General! General!"

~

Far above, Greeley's hovercraft remained silent. The general sat in quiet contemplation, his gaze fixed on the battle unfolding below. He finally turned to his assistant.

"Release the T.I.T.A.N."

The assistant nodded and swiftly tapped a sequence on the console.

With a mechanical hiss, the bay doors of the hovercraft slid open, revealing a massive object suspended in the darkness. It instantly dropped, plummeting toward the earth like a falling star. Flames ignited from its thrusters, roaring as it hurtled toward the ground with terrifying speed.

~

Acer glanced up, his eyes widening in anticipation. A wide grin spread across his face as the hulking shape descended, a promise of an overwhelming power now moments away.

With a thunderous crash, the object landed. The dust cleared, revealing:

~

Goliath—affectionately named but officially known as the Terrestrial Invasion Tactical Assault Nexus (or T.I.T.A.N.). A 20-foot-tall, towering war machine built for destruction. Its gleaming armor covered every surface, designed to protect and intimidate. Plasma cannons hummed with energy on its shoulders while missile pods and heavy guns along its arms waited to rain devastation. Inside the cockpit, the A.I. **NYX** (Neural Yaw and Execution System) monitored every system with incredible precision. Her calm voice guided the user of Goliath's moves, calculating the perfect moments to strike.

As it loomed over the plaza, the faint scent of new circuitry—the unmistakable "new hypercar smell" lingered in the air, a strange contrast to the cold, lethal purpose it embodied.

Acer didn't hesitate, climbing the ladder and slipping into the cockpit. The canopy was sealed with a pressurized hiss, enclosing him in metal. As his hands gripped the controls, a surge of power pulsed through the machine. Suddenly, spinning lasers filled the cockpit with crisscrossing beams, scanning him from head to toe. The beams pulsed rapidly, synchronizing his movements with Goliath's systems. Each pass of the lasers brought a tighter connection, the machine responding to him like an extension of his body. The hum of the engines vibrated through the frame, merging with the rhythmic sweep of the lasers. Nyx flickered onto the heads-up display, her voice calm and steady.

"Scanning complete. All systems nominal, Commander Acer," she confirmed, as the lasers finished syncing.

From his elevated position inside the towering mech, Acer looked down at Saar, now a tiny figure lost in the vast plaza. The scale difference was striking. A grin spread across Acer's face as confidence surged, his weapon now entirely under his command.

This time, Saar wouldn't escape.

Torn the Heart Out

Acer stood at the controls inside Goliath, the mech's sensors glowing like watchful eyes, tracing his every motion. He lifted his arms with purpose, and the massive exoskeleton mimicked the movement, its systems amplifying his voice.

"THE DOCTOR IS IN! READY FOR YOUR HEART TRANSPLANT?!" Acer's voice boomed, the sarcasm projected through the machine's speakers.

~

What the hell, Zoe?

Zoe's response came steady, almost casual.

That is T.I.T.A.N., An early mech prototype. It paved the way for some of your upgrades.

The cannons on Goliath's shoulders began to hum, red energy building up. Acer pulled the triggers, unleashing twin blasts of scorching EMPs. Saar dodged just in time, the red beams striking and obliterating the vehicles behind him. He rolled and sprang back up, dodging blast after blast as the ground erupted with burning debris. Acer kept the pressure on, his grin growing wider with each near miss, forcing Saar closer to the church's entrance.

~

Across the street, Jay edged nearer, trying to get a better view. His eyes were sharp, his breath shallow, as the battle unfolded before him.

~

Inside the church, refugees of various faiths gathered in the pews, the thick walls muffling most of the chaos outside. Some clutched each other in fear, while others, drained from days of turmoil, had fallen into restless sleep. Murmurs of uncertainty drifted through the church space.

A little girl, no more than six, stirred where she lay, her mother still asleep beside her. Drawn by the distant sounds of conflict, she stood up and wandered to the heavy doors. No one noticed as her small hands found the handle. Beyond the thick walls, a muffled voice rumbled through.

"GET READY FOR SOME REAL POWER!"

Acer's voice boomed from Goliath, its force rattling the walls around her.

Without hesitation, the girl pulled the door open. Her eyes widened in shock as she saw Saar, his back turned, standing between her and the massive Goliath. The towering machine loomed just feet away, its cannons locked on Saar, ready to fire. A sharp, terrified scream escaped her, slicing through the air like a siren.

"Look out!" Jay shouted, pointing frantically at the girl.

Then, time seemed to slow.

Saar spun, his gaze locking on the child.

The girl's mother woke with a frantic scream, rushing from the pews—too late.

The blast had fired before Saar could react. His body moved on instinct, fueled by sheer desperation. With a burst of speed, he hurled himself toward the girl, scooping her into his arms just as the searing energy beam cut through the air behind them. The force of the blast rumbled past, narrowly missing them before slamming into the heart of the church. The pews erupted in an explosion, splintering into jagged fragments. Shards of wood and debris tore through, like shrapnel, raining down on the terrified refugees. Their screams reverberated through the hollowed-out space, mingling with the deafening sound of destruction. In the chaos, some lives were extinguished instantly, swallowed by the wreckage.

Saar slammed into the ground, skidding to a halt with the crying girl held tightly against his chest. Gently, he let her go, guiding her back to her frantic, sobbing mother. The air rang with the cries of survivors, but Saar's focus had already shifted. Goliath loomed ahead, poised for more destruction. His gaze locked onto the massive mech, his resolve sharpening. He had to stop it—no matter what.

Inside the mech, Acer scowled, his frustration mounting as he slammed another button.

"Prep the big guns," he snapped at the A.I.

Nyx initiated the sequence to power up Goliath's guns.

The path was clear now. Goliath stomped forward through the gaping church entrance, each step crushing what remained of the sanctuary. Acer gestured impatiently, like Bruce Lee, taunting Saar to face him.

Flesh and Nanoceramic Steel

Jay slipped behind the moving mech, crouching as low as possible, his eyes darting between the destruction and the towering machine that had ripped the heart out of the church.

The sanctuary, once a place of refuge, was now a ruin—thick smoke, shattered stone, and bodies scattered across the floor. The cries of the wounded echoed through the air, mingling with the sharp smell of burning wood.

Jay dropped to his knees beside a still figure, but the vacant eyes staring back told him it was too late. His jaw tightened, fists trembling as he pressed them against the cold floor.

Across the church, Goliath moved like a juggernaut, its massive frame crushing everything in its path. Saar hid, watched from the shadows, waiting for the right moment to strike. His body tensed, fury building. In one swift motion, he charged, his body a blur of movement as he hurled himself toward the towering mech.

Inside the cockpit, Nyx calculated Saar's movements, and Acer swiftly raised the mech's foot, ready to bring it down to the precise spot where Saar was predicted to be.

The mech's leg came down hard, but Saar reacted faster. He caught the giant foot with both hands, servos whirring as his enhanced strength held the immense weight at bay. The floor buckled beneath Saar, struggling under the force. It seemed Goliath would win for the moment, but Saar's systems hummed with power as he pushed back. Bit by bit, the massive mech began to tilt. With one final surge, Saar sent Goliath crashing onto its metal ass. The impact rocked the church, sending clouds of dust and debris spiraling into the air.

Inside Goliath, Acer was also thrown on his ass, though the restraints kept him from injuring himself. Furious, he hammered the controls.

"Get me back up," he yelled.

~

Meanwhile, Saar caught up with Jay.

"Are you all right?" Saar asked.

Jay nodded. "I'm good."

Saar, poised to spring into action, felt Jay's hand clamp around his arm.

"Hey, man," Jay continued, "I was wrong about you. I'm sorry."

Saar paused, the word "man" lingering in his mind. Did that label still apply to him?

"Get these people out of here, officer," Saar said.

Saar sprinted away, weaving through the debris while directing some survivors toward the exit.

~

Inside the downed mech, Acer gritted his teeth, his face twisted with frustration. He slammed his fists against the command panel, forcing Goliath to respond. The machine groaned, its internal systems flickering with power as it struggled to rise. Slowly, the giant mech began to push itself upright, shaking off the rubble clinging to its metal shell. The sound of creaking metal filled the air as the massive machine strained against the debris. Though battered and battle-scarred, Goliath was far from defeated.

Saar, catching the movement out of the corner of his eye, turned just as Goliath stood tall once more. Its armor was dented, smoke curling from exposed wiring, but the mech's menacing presence was undeniable. Acer's snarl echoed through the cockpit as Goliath repositioned, ready to fight again.

"YOU'RE GONNA PAY FOR THAT, JUNKPILE!" Acer's voice thundered through the church.

Saar didn't waver. He sprinted toward Goliath and leaped onto the windshield, his hands gripping the glass tightly, extruded fingernails digging into the surface.

His eyes locked with Acer's, their mutual hatred palpable in the charged space between them. With a grim determination, Saar's hand shifted, nanobots transforming it into a heavy hammer. He raised it and brought it down against the cockpit window. Each blow reverberated through the church, the reinforced glass buckling under the relentless assault. Soon, a crack snaked across the surface, deepening with every strike.

Acer's confidence faltered, for a moment, but he quickly made a "grab-a-bug-from-your-face" gesture. Instantly, Goliath's arm shot up, mirroring the movement. The mech's massive hand clamped down on Saar, ripping him from the windshield and hurling him across the church like a discarded toy. Saar flew through the air, smashing through the pews, wooden splinters erupting in all directions. He tumbled to a stop near the altar, just feet away from the thick rope that led up to The Peacemaker overhead.

~

Jay, still helping people to safety, glanced back in time to see Saar thrown away like garbage. His voice cut through the panic, directing people toward the back.

"Keep moving! Keep moving! This way!"

In the chaos, Jay's eyes caught a familiar figure. Andre, wrapped in clean blankets, stood trembling with fear, lost in the crowd.

"Andre!" Jay shouted, his heart leaping with a mix of relief and worry.

Andre turned, eyes wide with relief.

"Jay! Thank God you're alive!"

They embraced briefly, overwhelmed by the moment.

"I thought you were gone," Jay said.

Andre shook his head, emotion welling in his eyes. "I thought so, too."

"Come on, let's get you out of here."

"I lost my dog—Diggity," Andre stammered. "She's gone."

"No. She's safe. I brought her to a friend."

Before Andre could respond, the ground shook as Goliath moved through the wreckage, scanning for Saar. Jay turned, urgency flooding him.

"Go! We'll find each other later."

Andre gave a grateful nod and vanished into the crowd.

~

Goliath's arm lashed out, seizing Saar by the leg. It hoisted him into the air, leaving him dangling upside down like a snared fish.

"YOU'RE GOING MAKE A NICE PAPERWEIGHT," Acer growled through Goliath's speakers.

Suddenly, POP! TINK! POP! TINK! POP! TINK!

Shots rang out, ricocheting off Goliath's windshield. Jay stood at a distance, pistol in hand, each bullet further splintering the cockpit glass, weakening it with every hit.

"Put him down, dickhead!" Jay yelled.

Goliath's arm transformed into a flamethrower and a wall of fire burst toward Jay. He dove to the ground, narrowly avoiding the blaze. The flames crackled and roared, triggering something deep within Jay—a memory. His body froze as images of a burning building flashed in his mind: the heat, the smoke, and the sound of a boy calling for help.

Paralyzed by guilt, Jay whispered, "I'm sorry…"

As Saar dangled upside down, he shouted, "Jay! Snap out of it!"

But Jay was trapped in the past, unmoving as the fire raged around him.

Saar clenched his fists and twisted free, somersaulting from Goliath's grip. He landed firmly on his feet, energy coursing through his body. Without a second thought, he revved his arm cannon and unleashed a focused blast straight at Goliath's cracked windshield. The glass shattered with a deafening CRACK, and the mech stumbled backward, toppling again.

~

Meanwhile, Saar rushed to Jay's side, shaking him.

"Snap out of it, Jay!"

"I tried…" Jay was lost in his guilt. "I'm sorry…"

Saar grabbed him again, more forcefully this time.

"It's me! Wake up!"

Finally, Jay's eyes cleared, reality flooding back in.

"What… what?"

"You need to get out of here," Saar said urgently, glancing at the flames creeping closer.

Jay, still dazed, wobbled as he tried to stand. Without hesitation, Saar hoisted him over his shoulder and sprinted toward the church's entrance. Reaching the back doors, he gently set Jay down, ensuring he was stable.

"Go," Saar said. "I'll handle this."

Jay started to protest, but Saar was already running back into the chaos.

Back inside the church, Goliath stood once more, its cannons glowing hot as it advanced on Saar—Acer, furious and relentless, locked onto his target. Saar leaped into the air.

Acer anticipated the move and swung Goliath's fist in a vicious arc. It struck hard, sending Saar crashing into the altar, shattering it. He hit the floor, dazed.

Suddenly, Zoe's voice crackled in Saar's ear.

Warning: minor shock to your organic implant.

Saar winced. "Not now."

Warning: minor shock to organic implant.

"I said not now!"

Zoe's voice cut out, and Saar's vision blurred as he looked up. Goliath loomed over him, cannons aimed directly at his chest.

"I've got orders to keep your noggin intact," Acer said, his voice stripped of Goliath's amplification. "But the rest of you? I'm going to turn into metal toothpicks."

Saar, summoning the last of his strength, fired his plasma guns at Goliath. The shots went wide, streaking past the mech and hurtling toward the ceiling.

Acer laughed. "Nice try, you bag of bolts!"

Acer primed his guns for one final shot, ready to end it. But before he could pull the trigger, the church bell rang out with a deep, ominous tone as Saar's projectiles slammed into it. The impact sent a violent tremor through the bell tower, snapping free from its headstock and yoke. The bell ripped free from its frame, its immense weight sending it crashing down with a thunderous roar.

The massive bell plunged, striking Goliath dead center with a crushing blow. The mech crumpled under the impact, metal twisting and bones snapping as flesh was crushed beneath the immense weight. One final, resonant tone rang out from the bell as it crashed, echoing through the church, shaking the walls and rattling the air. Acer's final shot was never fired.

The bell's final tone faded, never to ring again.

~

Saar, battered and torn, lay on the ground, staring at the aftermath around him. He pushed himself up slowly, limping past the wreckage of the fallen mech. His eyes found Jay, who managed a weary smile from across the room. They exchanged a silent moment of shared victory before Saar's legs gave out. He collapsed, face-first, into the rubble. Jan ran to him as fast as he could.

He knelt beside Saar, his heart pounding. "Stay with me, Saar. Stay with me."

Saar groaned, his cyborg frame shuddering from the damage. Jay steadied him, his hand coming away slick with blue, viscous fluid seeping from the head wound.

"What's going on?" Jay asked.

Saar struggled to speak, his voice crackling through failing vocal circuits.

"Don't... know," he rasped. "Zoe! What's... wrong... with me?"

Saar alone heard the burst of static as Zoe's voice crackled to life in his mind.

Analyzing... A brief pause followed before she continued. *Detected a severe crack in your Cerebral Fluid Containment Module. You're losing crucial neurofluids. Your implant is failing.*

"What's happening?" Jay asked.

Saar's voice dropped to a faint whisper.

"The sphere containing my brain—is leaking. Zoe says I'm losing fluids."

Saar turned his focus back to the A.I.

Zoe, fix it.

The damage can be repaired, Zoe responded, *however, the necessary materials are not readily available.*

Saar's body shuddered. "How long do I have?"

Thirty-four minutes, six seconds, and counting, Zoe said.

Jay, unable to hear Zoe, saw Saar's pained expression. "What did she say?"

Saar, struggling to stay conscious, repeated Zoe's message. Jay's mind raced, panic setting in.

"Thirty-four minutes? Well… we need to get these materials. Where do we get them?" Jay asked.

Saar's eyes flickered, his focus shifting inward as he silently communicated with Zoe.

"Zoe says… AICO… South… the complex housing… Project 24."

Jay's heart sank under the crushing weight of the situation. But then, an idea struck him.

"That's just a few minutes away from here. We can get there in time and get the materials you need."

Determination surged through Jay. His fingers fumbled desperately as he reached for his radio. The emergency frequencies should still be working topside."Delta twenty-five, on a ten-ninety-nine, at the Grand Mass Church. Officer needs assistance. I repeat—"

Before he could finish, Saar's hand shot up, crushing the radio in his grip. Even in his weakened state, his strength was undeniable. Jay stared, shocked, as the shattered pieces fell to the ground.

"Why'd you do that?!"

"They will hear you and… kill you," Saar rasped.

Jay met his gaze, disbelief and frustration burning in his chest.

"Then how in the hell can I save you?!"

"Don't… worry about me. Save… her."

Fueled by anger, Jay forced himself to his feet, using every bit of strength to lift Saar with him. As they hobbled toward the shattered church doors, Saar sagged heavily against him, growing weaker with each step.

~

The cold air hit them like a wall as they stumbled outside, only to be met with a sight that made Jay's blood run cold.

An entire platoon of about 30 soldiers stood in their way, photon rifles gleaming under the harsh light of hovering drones. Three unmanned tanks loomed behind them, cannons trained on them.

"Shit…" Jay muttered.

Lines Drawn

General Greeley stood at the front of the formation, an unlit cigar clamped between his teeth. His eyes glinted with amusement as he surveyed the scene.

"My God!" The general's gravelly voice boomed out. "You truly are a phenomenon, 23. You've impressed us all beyond our wildest expectations. Even the goddamn Special Forces couldn't handle you," he said with a chuckle.

Saar sagged against Jay, barely conscious, his body trembling with every breath.

"Let's go home, soldier," Greeley continued. "You've done well."

Saar clenched his jaw, summoning the last of his strength.

"Go to hell," he muttered, barely above a whisper.

"What did you say?" Greeley asked.

"I said... NO!"

Jay cut in.

"Ah... excuse me. General Dickhead? Yeah. You. He's not going with you! He's coming with me."

Greeley's gaze snapped to Jay.

"This doesn't concern you, Officer Mauritius."

"The hell it doesn't."

"You're out of your jurisdiction."

"Everything I'm standing on is my jurisdiction."

Saar stirred, his voice barely audible.

"Jay... don't..."

"Shut up," Jay whispered.

"What you've got there," Greeley said, "is government property. He's a machine—built, engineered, and designed by the United States Army. Every piece of metal, every synthetic part, and every drop of fluid in his system belongs to us."

"He's not property," Jay said. "He's human."

Greeley's eyes narrowed.

"I don't know what he's told you," Greeley said, "but whatever it is, it's just part of his programming. He's hardwired to manipulate and deceive to get what he wants."

Jay paused, considering the possibility. He knew Saar was fully capable of manipulation, as his programming allowed for it, and Saar could easily deceive if it meant survival or achieving his goal. But something deep inside gnawed at him, a gut feeling that refused to align with logic. Despite everything he knew, something about Saar's demeanor and desperation made Jay believe this time was different. Whatever it was, Saar was the genuine article.

"He's more human than you or I will ever be," Jay said.

Saar's eyes fluttered open momentarily, a flicker of gratitude passing through them.

"Officer? He's a property," he yelled. "Once again. You're interfering with U.S. military operations! Move out of the way!"

Jay stood his ground, unwavering.

Greeley's patience wore thin; his jaw clenched so hard around the cigar it almost snapped in half. Without turning, he barked the order:

"Lieutenant!"

The General stepped aside as the lieutenant marched forward, already knowing what was expected. He spun to face the assembled troops.

"Present arms!" The Lieutenant barked.

Photon rifles snapped upright, barrels pointing toward the sky in a precise display of discipline.

"Aim!"

In unison, the soldiers lowered their weapons, now aiming squarely at Jay and Saar, fingers hovering over the triggers, ready to fire immediately.

Before the inevitable could unfold, the sharp wail of distant sirens sliced through the tense standoff. Within moments, flashing lights appeared on the horizon as a convoy of police vehicles roared into the plaza, quickly encircling the platoon, their sheer numbers overwhelming the military force.

Captain Bennett stepped out, her face unreadable as she approached Jay.

"Disregarded orders again, I see," she said.

Jay's relief was palpable.

"My last call went through."

Bennett nodded slightly. She glanced at Saar, her brow furrowing.

"What's with him?"

"We need a police escort to AICO South. Right now. All I ask is that you trust me."

Bennett considered it for a moment, then nodded. "Done."

"You're not seriously considering this end-of-career decision, are you, Captain?!" Greeley said.

Bennett turned toward the general, who stood near the platoon. She fixed him with a steady stare, completely unfazed.

"You and your men are out of line, General," she said.

Greeley's face flushed red with barely concealed rage.

The General lifted his hand, a silent command that sent the troops into a tense, ready-to-fire stance, their weapons trained on Bennett.

"This isn't a discussion," he warned.

Bennett, unshaken, raised her hand high in a gesture of solidarity. Her officers instantly responded as one, drawing their weapons with precision that only years of trust and camaraderie could build. The unmistakable click of safeties disengaging echoed in perfect unison, a silent declaration that they stood together, unbreakable. The army platoon shifted uneasily, sensing the unspoken bond of the police force—a brotherhood, a sisterhood, ready to face anything as one.

The General flinched; his composure cracked for a split second.

Meanwhile, with determination, Jay helped Saar into the back of a Talon, then quickly slid into the driver's seat. The engine roared to life, vibrating with the moment's urgency, ready to tear down the road.

Greeley's hand hovered near his sidearm. "You won't like how this ends," he warned Bennett.

Bennett stood firm with her officers ready, eyes locked on Greeley. For a moment, the world seemed to hold its breath.

As the standoff persisted, Greeley's VoxLink buzzed in his pocket. His eyes flicked upward briefly, catching sight of one of the drones hovering above, its lens reflecting the scene below. Whoever was on the other end of the line was watching. The General glanced at the device, his anger slowly dissolving into something colder and more calculating.

Without hesitation, Greeley answered the call. His words were clipped, the exchange brief but tense. The conversation carried weight, though knowing exactly what had been said was impossible.

When he hung up, his expression was unreadable, a practiced mask of control. His gaze briefly shifted back to the drone above, an unspoken acknowledgment of the unseen power watching over them all.

"Fall back," Greeley commanded.

The soldiers hesitated, clearly confused, but obeyed. Their guns lowered.

Jay wasted no time, slamming the Talon into gear and speeding off, with a line of police cruisers close behind, their lights flashing and sirens piercing the night. Some officers tailed him, while others remained with Bennett, holding their ground in the tense standoff. Jay glanced in the rearview mirror, watching as part of the force stayed behind, knowing the situation was still far from over. But right now, every second mattered, and he had to focus on getting Saar to safety.

Greeley knew when to back off, but not without one last attempt to assert his dominance. He stared down Bennett, his gaze hard and cold, trying to intimidate her. She didn't flinch. As the convoy sped off, Greeley's expression darkened. Without turning, he barked a command to a nearby soldier.

"Private! Go scrape Commander Acer off the church floor."

Fragile Alliance

Hours later, the night skies remained still as General Greeley's hover vehicle floated above the locked-down city, a sleek silhouette against the dark expanse.

~

Inside the vehicle, from his command chair, the general surveyed the endless data streams scrolling across his console. An enormous screen before him cast a soft glow, displaying a picturesque view of the pristine metropolis below—its towering spires and shimmering lights forming an architectural marvel. Yet, it was only a screensaver—a peaceful facade hiding the storm brewing beneath.

At the controls, one of his assistants worked silently, fingers tapping frantically against the interface, as if sheer effort could dispel the tension in the air. The hum of machinery was the only sound until the assistant turned, his voice hesitant.

"Sir? Chancellor Bellwether, on the secured channel."

It was an "oh, shit" moment. The General composed himself quickly, leaning back in his chair, an unlit cigar at the ready.

"Put him on."

The assistant tapped the screen, and the serene cityscape vanished, replaced by the stern face of Quadrant Overseer Steven Bellwether, head of the Washington Quadrant. He was known for never missing a crack or flaw in his domain. Every wrinkle on his face was carved by decades of political maneuvering, but for now, his gray hair was standing stiff with irritation. His sharp, icey voice cut through the air like a freshly honed blade.

"What the hell is going on, General?"

Greeley waved his hand, dismissing his assistant, who hurried out of the room without a second glance. The door hissed shut, leaving the two men alone in their tense exchange. Greeley held the unlit cigar between his fingers.

"What now, Chancellor?"

"You know damn well 'what now,'" Bellwether said. "Project 23 is in police custody?! How did that happen? Do you have any idea how much structural damage was caused? How many civilians were killed?"

Greeley's face remained impassive, but his grip tightened on the unlit cigar.

"I don't know what you mean, Chancellor. We only target military installations, not civilians."

"Are you insane?! There were civilian casualties—residents of New Sinai, in a church, for God's sake!"

The Chancellor's fury battered Greeley like waves pounding a stubborn rock, relentless but never breaking him. He stayed composed, calmly inspecting his cigar —like a stone smoothed by water over time, it had made him more patient, not weaker.

"No need to worry, Chancellor. They're delivering 23 right to us. I'm not letting some no-name cop ruin what took 15 years to build. You're overreacting."

Bellwether's face flushed an even darker red, the veins at his temples standing out like strained cords.

"Overreacting?! Do you even understand what's on the line here? Convincing the media to swallow the terrorists' and Far Right's garbage was the easy part. But how am I supposed to deal with the police? They've got their prejudices, but they're not idiots."

Greeley sniffed his cigar, slow and deliberate, savoring the moment.

"Propaganda," Greeley said, "is your specialty, not mine."

Bellwether's voice stayed cool.

"The first thing we do is wipe away every mistake you've made before the media gets a hold of it. Every article, every file, every witness—erased. We make it disappear. The police, the press, anyone who tries to dig into this? They're shut down, no questions asked."

"How exactly do you plan to pull that off? You can't make a whole city forget."

Leaning closer to the screen, Bellwether's tone dropped into a dangerous whisper.

"Don't be so sure, General. We control the narrative. Shut down communication, throw confusion into the mix, and undercut the cops before they can connect the dots. In the meantime, I've got an army of my own. They tie up the loose ends."

Greeley's smirk faded as he realized how far Bellwether was willing to go. He tapped on his unlit cigar, flicking imaginary ashes.

"You're talking about a cover-up on a massive scale."

"This isn't about damage control anymore. It's about survival. Just do your job, and I'll do mine. Got it?"

The screen flickered, then went dark. The Chancellor was gone, leaving the ambiance to settle back into the room. Greeley sat motionless, his eyes locked on the blank screen.

After a long moment, he reached for the guillotine cutter, slicing the head off the cigar with deliberate precision.

Asshole!

He bit down on the cigar, lit it, and watched the tip flicker to life. A quiet satisfaction settled over him as the smoke he exhaled hung in the air before moving away.

Beneath the Flames

The I-95 South corridor that sliced through New Sinai stretched beneath the night, a dark ribbon disappearing into the horizon. Above, the sky was a deep indigo dotted with distant stars, silent witnesses to the world below. The highway, eerily empty under the curfew, seemed frozen in time, as the hours before sunrise crept in, casting a faint glow on the horizon, hinting at the day's arrival.

A convoy of police vehicles, their red and blue lights flashing, raced behind Jay's Talon down the empty highway. The desolate road flickered with each light pulse, casting animated shadows across the pavement. They moved in perfect rhythm, as if they weren't just after criminals but something far more sinister lurking beneath.

~

Jay's hands clamped onto the steering wheel, knuckles turning pale as his jaw locked tight. His eyes were fixed on the stretch of asphalt ahead, and the road was the only thing keeping his thoughts from spiraling out of control. Behind him, Saar slouched in the back seat, silent as ever, a reminder of the time slipping away. Jay's VoxLink sat lifeless on the passenger seat, its dark screen mocking him. The messages he'd left for his wife remained unanswered, each one weighing heavier than the last.

He had tried more than once to reach her, leaving messages of apology, promising that this time would be different—that he would be different. He had asked her to meet him halfway, but now, all he had was silence. And with every tick of the clock, doubt gnawed at him. Maybe it was already too late.

The quiet between them lingered until Saar finally broke it, his voice softer than usual.

"Back at the church... why'd you freeze like that?"

Jay didn't respond right away. His grip on the wheel tightened as he dragged himself back to the present. But the question burrowed into him, forcing memories to rise to the surface, ones he'd spent years trying to bury.

"I've got PTSD," he said at last, his voice strained. "Post-Traumatic Stress Disorder."

Saar hesitated before asking, "What happened?"

Jay's heart thudded in his chest. He didn't want to open up, didn't want to revisit the darkest part of his past. But it bubbled up anyway, unstoppable. He needed a release.

"A few years ago," he started slowly, "I'd been on the force for just a couple of years. There was this massive apartment fire—five alarms. We were called to block off streets, keep the crowd back so the firefighters could work. But this fire was like something alive: Flames swallowed everything, and smoke was so thick it choked you just standing nearby. Even the firefighters couldn't get in."

His grip on the wheel loosened as the memory took hold, pulling him away from the present moment.

"There was this woman on the sidewalk, screaming for her kid. No one seemed to notice her—too much chaos, too many people to help. And then we saw him." Jay blinked hard, his eyes burning. "He was at the window, a little boy, helpless. His mother collapsed right there on the street when she saw him. I begged the firefighters to do something, but they couldn't. The building was on the verge of collapsing."

Saar stayed quiet, just listening.

"I ran into the building and up the stairs. Smoke was everywhere. I couldn't hear him at first, but then—there was a voice, sounded terrified. I kicked a door open, and there he was, hiding under a table, flames all around. I grabbed him, wrapped him in a blanket, and tried to get us out. But the way I had come in was blocked. I headed for the back exit, but then a burning beam crashed down in front of us."

Jay's hands shook on the wheel. His voice trembled as the words came out, slow and heavy.

"I had to set him down for just a second, just long enough to move the beam. It was heavy and on fire, and I knew my hands would burn, but I didn't care. The adrenaline kept me going. I shoved the beam aside. And then… I heard it."

Jay wiped his eyes with the back of his hand, but the pain didn't go away. It stayed, like an ember that refused to burn out.

"I turned around, and the floor was gone. And… so was he."

After a long pause, Saar spoke again.

"What was his name?"

The boy's gravesite flickered in his mind, surfacing without warning. It was the place he had visited every week since that day.

"Christopher," Jay said. "Christopher Wright."

A Snowy Place

Minutes had passed in somber silence. Jay tightened his grip on the wheel, eyes fixed on the road as the early light clawed its way through the fading night. The Talon rumbled beneath him.

Saar shifted slightly, his voice breaking the silence.

"Fear is necessary... for survival," Saar said, "It's woven into the human experience. It triggers your... fight or flight. Keeps your kind alive."

Jay didn't reply immediately. His mind wandered, dragged back to memories he'd rather leave buried.

"Sometimes…," Saar continues, "fear takes control. Turns into something bigger. In your case... fire."

"Yeah," Jay said, "But what should I do about it?"

"Face it. Fire isn't the enemy... fear is."

"It's not that simple."

Their eyes met in the rearview mirror. Saar's face had grown paler, his energy visibly draining.

"When you stop fearing the fire," Saar said, "you'll face the real scars—guilt and remorse."

The weight of Saar's words hit Jay hard. He'd always thought it was the fire itself—the chaos, the heat, the destruction—that haunted him. But now, it was clear. The fire was just a mask. What he really feared was the guilt that came with it, the reminder that he had failed. That he hadn't saved Christopher. His grip loosened, his breath unsteady. It wasn't the flames that kept him up at night—it was the guilt, the endless replaying of choices he couldn't change. And until he faced that, the fire would always have power over him.

But as the truth settled in, another worry surfaced. He glanced back at Saar, concerned.

"How you holding up?" Jay asked, sensing the strain in Saar's movements.

"Not great... My electrical systems are stabilizing, but... the fluids are depleting. My brain... is starving."

"Just hold on." Jay said, "We're almost there."

The minutes dragged on, each mile stretching longer than the last.

This time, Jay broke the silence.

"Does she have a name?"

Saar tilted his head slightly, as if the question caught him off guard.

"A name?"

"Yeah. Calling her Project 24 feels... artificial. You guys can pick your own names, right?"

"We do," Saar replied slowly. "We choose our names."

"Maybe it's time you gave her one, too. Something more... human."

Saar turned to the window, watching the dawn light streak the sky in gold and crimson. His eyes lingered on the horizon, his thoughts distant.

"Something human..." he murmured.

"A name should mean something," Jay added.

Saar remained quiet, staring ahead. Jay's words hadn't quite sunk in yet. After a pause, he spoke again, his voice softer.

"Jay, I've been... seeing things."

"Seeing things? Like what?"

"Images," Saar said. "During downtime. They just... come to me."

"Sounds like you're having dreams."

"Dreams?" Saar echoed, as if trying to understand the word. "Is that what dreams are?"

"Sure. You've got a human brain. Dreams probably come with the package."

Saar stayed quiet, his gaze still fixed ahead.

"I… dream… of a snowy place… cold, white, but bright. She was there. And so was I. We were happy together."

Jay wasn't one to put much weight into dreams; they always seemed like scattered fragments from a restless mind. He didn't quite know how to respond, or why it seemed to matter so much to Saar. He focused on the road, unsure of where it was all leading, but he could sense there was something deeper to Saar's experience that he couldn't fully grasp.

The Iron Gauntlet

The convoy surged forward, engines rumbling like a beast in pursuit. Jay's Talon rattled as it sped over the cracked pavement, his eyes locked on the distant gates of AICO South. It was a fortress of carbonmatrix concrete and nanoceramic steel, crawling with soldiers. The police escort held their formation, but something in Jay's gut felt wrong.

Up ahead, soldiers in full combat gear stood blocking the entrance. Tanks lined the sides, drones buzzed overhead, their weapons aimed at the convoy. Two massive drone gunships circled in the sky, their mini-guns angled toward the ground, while smaller attack drones hovered nearby. Every possible way out was cut off.

Behind him, Saar stirred, moving like a malfunctioning machine just waking up. His mechanical body seemed sluggish, but his mind raced, running calculations at a speed that blurred thought. He was in constant communication with Zoe.

Jay glanced at Saar before turning his attention back to the blockade. His knuckles whitened around the wheel.

"This isn't good," he muttered, grabbing the radio. "DT25. Code 22. Everyone pull back. Find cover."

The convoy came to a halt several yards behind Jay. The police scrambled out of their cars, taking shelter behind the vehicles, readying themselves for what was coming.

Jay's Talon coasted through the front gate, suspiciously left open, and skidded to a stop. Silence hung for a beat before the compound's loudspeakers crackled to life, and General Greeley's voice boomed out.

"You have one minute to hand over the AWOL soldier. If you refuse, we open fire."

Jay grimaced. "He's bluffing," he said, though it felt more like a hope than a fact.

"Don't count on it," Saar replied, pointing weakly at the dashboard. "That switch. When I say flip it? Flip it!"

Jay's eyes darted to the switch. The red cover had already been snapped open. His hand hovered over it, uncertainty crawling in.

"Thirty seconds!" Greeley's voice echoed across the compound.

Saar straightened, his expression hardening. "Get ready."

Jay's heart pounded, his finger hovering above the switch.

"10-9-8-7-6..."

"Now!" Saar yelled.

Jay slammed the switch down. The sunroof hissed open, and the roof-mounted fifty-caliber machine gun rose into position. Saar grabbed hold and unleashed a burst of fire. The heavy rounds ripped through the air, hammering the nearest drone gunship.

The drone lurched, its rotors shredded, and crashed into the second gunship. Both spiraled out of control, erupting into flames as they hit the ground, sending soldiers scrambling for cover. Panic spread through the ranks as fire and debris rained down.

"Forward!" Saar barked.

Jay hesitated, his gaze locked on the inferno ahead. Flames roared, dancing wildly as debris scattered across the compound. The fire reflected in his eyes, flickering like the doubt that gripped him. For a moment, the world seemed to slow—chaos swirling just beyond the windshield—while he sat frozen, unsure if they'd make it through.

"Jay! Now! Move!"

Jay snapped out of it, adrenaline surging as he stomped on the gas. The Talon lunged forward, charging straight into the wall of flames. Heat engulfed the car, the fire blurring his vision, searing against the windshield. For a heartbeat, it felt like they might be swallowed whole, but just as quickly, they burst through the blaze, emerging into the clear beyond.

A surge of relief flooded Jay's chest. The roar of the fire faded behind them, replaced by the cool rush of open air. For the first time in a long while, he felt a quiet sense of triumph, like he'd stared down something that had haunted him and won. The hesitation, the doubt—it didn't matter anymore. He had pushed through.

Moments later, the smaller attack drones dove in, their guns lighting up the sky. Saar opened fire without hesitation, his aim precise. One after another, the drones shattered in midair, erupting into fireballs as their remains scattered across the compound like falling shrapnel.

"Keep moving!" Saar shouted.

Jay needed no more prompting. The Talon raced toward the entrance of AICO South, the ground strewn with the wreckage of downed drones. The fortress loomed nearer, its doors gaping like the jaws of a beast, ready to swallow them whole.

Betrayal

The Talon screeched to a stop in the narrow corridor, blocked by a nanoceramic steel barricade. Saar stumbled out, clutching his head as pain coursed through him. His face twisted in discomfort. Jay hurried after him, catching sight of Saar's strained expression.

"Saar?"

"It's... my head. Feels like it's splitting."

Jay glanced down the corridor, scanning for an exit or another threat.

"We have to hurry. Which way? We need to move."

Saar acted quickly, snapping one of Jay's handcuffs around his left wrist and fastening the other end to the Talon's driver's side-view mirror.

"What the—?" Jay tugged at the chain, panic rising in his chest. "Saar, what's going on? What are you doing?!"

Saar straightened, his face calm but distant. He reached for Jay's weapon, tossing it far away.

"I'm sorry."

"You can't leave me here! You need backup!"

Saar looked at him, his expression softening.

"You've done more than enough, officer. But this… this is something I have to finish alone."

Saar didn't wait for a reply. He turned and limped down the corridor, his silhouette slowly disappearing into the harsh, sterile light. Jay stood there, frozen and powerless.

~

Saar trudged through the labyrinthine corridors, each step slower, more unsteady than the last. It felt like he was moving through invisible resistance, his systems faltering, inching toward failure. Warnings blinked at the edges of his vision—circuits burning out, vital functions shutting down one by one—but he refused to stop. His servos groaned with every movement, and the once-fluid coordination of his mechanical joints had become jerky and uneven. Each step was a battle. Yet, something more profound than the synthetic drive in his body pushed him forward. It wasn't the programming or the mission etched into his code—it was a force beyond calculation, beyond any algorithm. This wasn't about survival. It was about finishing what he had started.

~

The door to the lab slid open with a soft hiss, revealing a cavernous room tangled in wires and glowing monitors. Scattered throughout were empty Cerebral Fluid Containment Modules—identical to the one that contained Saar's brain—lying hollow, their purposes long forgotten.

At the center of the room, suspended in a delicate network of life-support machines, lay Project 24.

Saar's synthetic eyes locked onto her, her body preserved in a fragile stasis, beautiful in a haunting, unnatural way. Her brain pulsed faintly inside a CFCM, connected to a delicate web of wires keeping her alive. Each tube, every thin connection, seemed vital—like threads holding onto a precarious existence, one that reflected Saar's own. The sight of her, untouched by the ravages of time, stirred something in him far deeper than any code-driven logic could explain.

Her skin was an eerie blend of synthetic material and fine porcelain, pale and unblemished, as if frozen in time. The delicate surface reminded Saar of an era long past, when craftsmen shaped fragile beauty into intricate designs, capturing an elusive sense of perfection. She seemed like something from another world—delicate, yet too pure to belong to this harsh reality.

Compelled, he took a step forward, his only thought to reach her. But as his hand stretched out, his body betrayed him. His failing systems locked up entirely, freezing him in place. He stood erect, locked in the anatomical position—arms stiff at his sides, legs rigid, unable to move. He fought against the paralysis, but his limbs felt impossibly heavy, as if an unseen force had seized control, holding him back from the one thing he couldn't bear to lose.

Zoe? His thoughts raced in panic. *What's happening to me?*

Unable to comply, Zoe's voice flickered in his mind, faint and distorted.

Zoe, override! Now!

General Greeley stepped forward from the shadows, his presence cold and commanding.

"Don't bother struggling," Greeley said, "Your A.I., your systems, your body—they're all under my control now."

Saar strained, fury surging through him as he fought against the unseen grip that held him still.

Zoe, override Greeley's commands! he demanded, desperation in his thoughts.

Unable to comply, Zoe said, her voice fading like a distant signal being lost.

Greeley smirked, circling Saar with the satisfaction of someone who knew victory was already his.

"You never truly understood your role in all of this, 23. But soon, you will."

The General's Gambit

Jay stretched awkwardly from the driver's seat, his reach strained by the chain linking him to the side mirror. His fingers fumbled inside the cramped glove compartment until they found cold metal. He grabbed the wrench, gripping it tightly. With little room to maneuver, he swung it at the chain, the impact sending a spray of sparks. Desperation fueled each strike, but the metal links barely showed a scratch, stubbornly holding him in place.

Out of breath, Jay stopped and stared at the cuffs biting into his wrist. The wrench was useless, and the chain seemed impossible to break. His eyes flicked toward the mirror, holding him captive like some cruel joke, and an idea took shape. If brute strength wasn't enough, maybe speed could do the trick.

~

In the cold confines of the lab, Saar stood frozen, his systems glitching, circuits flickering as if dying. General Greeley circled him like a predator savoring his power. The General's eyes gleamed with satisfaction.

"This isn't personal," Greeley said. "I'd rather keep you all intact. But if I can't…"

He spread his fingers wide in a mock explosion. Saar's gaze shifted, focusing on the explosives set neatly around Project 24's bed. Despite his locked joints, his mind raced faster, processing every detail.

"You and her," Greeley continued, pausing to admire his work, "you two are the best things to come from the Spear of Saar project. Did you know that?"

He stood inches from Saar now, his smile mocking.

"Nothing to say?" Greeley tilted his head, then chuckled, suddenly remembering. "Oh, right. I forgot—let's fix that."

With a tap on his HoloPad, the General sent a command. Saar felt a subtle shift in his face—the tight grip over his expressions loosened. His voice returned, though the rest of his body remained locked in place.

"You lied to us," Saar said. "You told us we were malfunctioning."

"Yep," Greeley replied.

"You planned to destroy us."

"Initially, yes," Greeley admitted, pacing again. "The engineers thought they knew better. Strip away your emotions, they said; make you more machine than man. But the mindless soldiers they ended up building? They were efficient, sure, but lacked something... critical."

He tapped the containment around Saar's brain as if to punctuate the point. His fondness for control was undeniable, and now, he was basking in the memory of proving just how vital Saar was.

"They didn't understand," Greeley continued. "When I sent you on that mission, it wasn't just to see if you'd follow orders. You were proving yourself—proving me right."

Greeley stopped, a proud gleam in his eyes as he remembered the mission's success.

"The brass didn't believe at first. They stood there, watching, skeptical as hell. But their doubt didn't last long when you tore through the enemy, one soldier at a time."

Saar felt Greeley's words creep into the edges of his thoughts, stirring old doubts. Had his hesitation during that mission—his moment of human vulnerability—been genuine? Or was it just more programming? The uncertainty gnawed at him.

"They couldn't deny it," Greeley said. "When it was over, you weren't just some experiment anymore. You were the future."

Greeley stepped closer, his tone lowering.

"That pause you had—the hesitation—wasn't a weakness. It was the thing that set you apart."

No. Saar pushed back against the creeping doubt. He wasn't a puppet—at least, not anymore. Greeley might have pulled the strings once, but Saar had cut himself loose. That hesitation, that flicker of humanity, wasn't something programmed into him. It was real. It was *him.*

"You and 23," Greeley said with finality, "you made them believe."

Saar's clarity sharpened. He wasn't disposable. He wasn't a puppet. He was free, and no one would ever control him again.

~

Jay slid into the Talon's driver's seat, looping the chain over the door as best he could. The cuffs bit into his wrist, the other end still tightly secured to the side mirror. His eyes locked on the carbonmatrix concrete barrier ahead. If he hit the right speed and angled the door perfectly, there was a chance the chain would snap.

Determined, he revved the engine, the Talon roaring to life beneath him. He sped forward, heart pounding, and with a sharp twist of the wheel, he angled the driver's side door toward the barrier. The impact came hard and fast, the door slamming shut with a jarring crash. The chain caught inside the door frame snapped in two.

The cuff remained clamped around his wrist, but he was free. Without wasting a second, Jay jumped out, grabbed his gun from the floor, and sprinted away.

~

Back in the lab, Greeley's pacing continued, oblivious to the chaos unfolding outside. Thick cables snaked down from the ceiling, latching onto the ports behind Saar's head, who sat motionless, his eyes vacant. Data streamed across Greeley's HoloPad, casting a faint glow.

"The Chancellor," Greeley said, "wanted a disciplined force—Quadrant enforcers bound by rules and protocols. A neat little army of obedient soldiers."

He sneered, shaking his head. "Order might keep things tidy, but it also slows you down. It makes you hesitate when there's no time for questions."

His tone grew colder, almost bitter. "But… I had a better idea. Soldiers who don't ask questions. Soldiers who act. Efficient. Relentless. Obedient."

He glanced at Saar, still paralyzed, a dark chuckle bubbling up.

"Do you know what he wanted to do?" He paused for effect. "Keep this quiet, but he eventually wanted to secede from the U.S. and become leader of his own nation." He laughed, shaking his head. "The man actually thought he could pull that off." His eyes narrowed, gleaming with ambition. "But if anyone's going to lead a charge like that, it should be me. I have the experience, I've got the vision— and… the army to make it happen."

Suddenly, alarms blared from the HoloPad. Greeley's face flickered with brief surprise.

"Hmm, your brain... it's degrading." He tapped commands on the screen. "Well, we can't have that."

A hiss filled the room as Saar's head cracked open, revealing the sphere protecting his brain. Tubes descended, pumping in a glowing blue fluid.

Saar's body twitched as the liquid coursed through him, but his mind sharpened, growing more defiant. Deep within, something unyielding resisted Greeley's control, refusing to give in.

Rebirth

Greeley watched Saar's containment globe fill, a smirk playing on his lips as the globe steadily filled.

"You should feel better soon," Greeley said, "We wouldn't want that brain of yours going to waste. It's the only part of you that matters."

Saar's eyes fluttered open, struggling to focus. His voice, barely above a whisper, cracked out a question,

"I feel weird," Saar muttered, his voice trembling. "What... what are you doing to me?"

"Feel? Weird?" Greeley chuckled. "Those are curious words coming from you. But no matter. We're going to extract your brain, vitrify it to preserve every detail, and then bioprint it, so that we can replicate it as many times as we need."

Saar's gaze sharpened.

"And what are you going to do to her?"

"Well," he said, "we really can't use her. We're thinking of putting her down."

For the first time, genuine fear crossed Saar's face. His eyes widened, the dread creeping in.

"No," he whispered.

His skin began to flush, the nanobots coursing through him, reacting to his anger.

Zoe, Saar called out within his mind, his voice desperate. *Let me go.*

I cannot.

Let me go! Saar demanded.

I cannot.

"No!" Saar's voice surged, his body vibrating with restrained power. Circuits flared beneath his synthetic skin, systems pushing against Zoe's control. Every line of code raced through his mind, forcing his processors into overdrive.

Release me, damnit! he demanded.

Greeley's smug expression faltered. He backed away, lifting his control HoloPad.

"23! What are you doing?"

"My name is not 23," Saar growled, his voice trembling with rage.

Greeley's fingers flew across the HoloPad, but every command flashed red— denied! Saar had taken control. He was rewriting the code in his own systems, overriding every function Greeley thought was locked down.

"That's... that's impossible," Greeley said, watching in disbelief as his system crumbled before him. "23, I said stop! That's an order!"

"My name is not 23," Saar shouted.

His entire body convulsed with energy, the blue liquid bubbling furiously through his veins. Though he had no heart, a rhythmic pulse—deep and unsettling —echoed within him. As the pressure built, Saar's vision dimmed, as he slipped into a dream.

He saw Jay racing into a burning building, flames devouring the structure. Inside, a child's cry pierced through the crackling fire. Without hesitation, Jay plunged through the smoke, finding the boy and pulling him into his arms, shielding him as they escaped the blaze. A strange, tightening beat pulsed within Saar when he saw the child's face—streaked with soot, eyes wide with terror. It was like staring into a reflection from years ago—his own face, his own fear, mirrored in the boy's helpless gaze.

The dream dissolved, and Saar was yanked violently back into reality. A sharp hiss filled the air as a laser torch descended toward him, aimed precisely at his neck. Its beam blazed, designed to sever his head cleanly without damaging the brain—preserving it perfectly intact. The heat pulsed closer, the beam nearly grazing his skin.

"23, you were never meant to have a choice," the General sneered.

***Saar's thoughts raced, fragments of Greeley's manipulations clawing at the edges of his mind. *You were never meant to have a choice*, Greeley had said. *That hesitation was what set you apart*, he'd insisted. For a moment, Saar questioned it—was that pause in his actions really a weakness? Or had it been his only truth in a sea of programming?

No! It wasn't doubt. It wasn't hesitation. That moment of hesitation was his—the flicker of humanity that had survived the machine. It wasn't code. It wasn't placed there by Greeley or anyone else.

It was him.

Saar's body tensed as rage boiled over. He locked eyes with the General.

"My name is **CHRISTOPHER**!" he roared.

With a final surge of power, Christopher ripped free from the cables. Sparks flew, and his eyes blazed with defiance as he glared at Greeley. In that instant, Zoe's presence vanished. The voice that had controlled him was gone. He stood on his own terms for the first time—free from her *and* free from Greeley.

In one fluid motion, Christopher slammed his forearm into Greeley's chest, sending him flying across the room. The general collided with the wall, collapsing as his HoloPad clattered to the floor. Gasping for breath, Greeley lay stunned, struggling to recover.

Christopher turned his attention to what mattered most: Project 24. His fingers trembled like a human's, brushing the cold synthetic skin of her cheek. It was strange—his body no longer needed to feel, yet in that moment, the sensation of her beneath his hand was more real than any mission he'd ever completed. Her eyes remained closed. He leaned in closer, his voice barely above a whisper.

"Aurora," he said softly, the name slipping out as though it had always been hers. "My dawn after the darkest night."

Slowly, her eyelids fluttered open, the soft glow of recognition flickering in her gaze. For a moment, her expression was one of confusion, as though she were waking from a dream, unsure of her place in the world. But then, she smiled—a small, hesitant curve of her lips—and repeated the name quietly, testing it, like a word she was just learning.

"Aurora," she echoed, her voice faint but warm.

Christopher's chest tightened—if he had a heart, it would have pounded. She was back. She was real.

He nodded, a smile tugging at his lips.

"Your new name."

Her smile deepened, a spark of life returning to her eyes. "I like that," she whispered, her fingers brushing his hand in quiet relief.

Aurora willed herself to move, but her limbs refused to obey.

"I... can't move."

Without hesitation, Christopher extended a connection pin from his forefinger and inserted it into the port at the base of her skull. His hands worked quickly as he began restoring her functions, his mind focused.

Behind them, Greeley, gasping for breath, managed to pull himself up. His hand fumbled for the fallen HoloPad, and he input a final command, his face twisted with grim satisfaction. He still had one last card to play.

As Christopher worked to revive Aurora, alarms blared suddenly throughout the facility. He whipped around just as the door exploded inward. Two dozen cyborgs flooded the room, each identical to him in face but disturbingly inhuman. Their eyes were vacant, betraying the absence of any real consciousness—their frames designed to house copies of Christopher's brain. Under the harsh lights, their skinless, metallic bodies gleamed, cold and efficient. Lacking the spark of life that came from a human mind, they moved as one—a soulless, unfeeling force driven solely by programming.

"Hold him down!" Greeley commanded.

Christopher unplugged from Aurora, pivoting swiftly as the first wave of cyborgs stormed in. His forearms shifted, his obedient nanobots forming to reveal photon cannons that hummed with raw energy. He aimed without hesitation, firing a series of quick, precise blasts. The first two cyborgs dropped instantly, sparks flying as their circuits fried.

But more surged forward, closing in from every direction. Christopher moved fast, targeting the closest, his shots clean and efficient. Yet their sheer numbers were relentless—each one identical to the last, cold and emotionless.

One leaped from behind, its hands locking onto his shoulders, pulling him back. Christopher spun, firing point-blank, the force sending the cyborg crashing into a nearby wall. Before he could fire another round, two more grabbed his arms, pinning them down, their grips like iron.

He struggled, his systems straining against the mechanical weight pressing him to the ground. More cyborgs piled on, their red eyes glowing as they overwhelmed him. The photon cannons dimmed, trapped beneath the crushing metal limbs.

Greeley lurched forward, clutching a portable laser torch. His face twisted with a cruel grin as he approached Christopher.

"A new name, how original," Greeley said. "But you're still just a cog in the machine."

The torch ignited with a sharp hiss.

"Hold him steady," Greeley ordered. "This needs to be clean."

As the torch neared Christopher's neck, its sharp hiss filled the air, the heat radiating against his skin. Greeley leaned in closer, a cruel smirk on his face, savoring the moment of victory. The red-hot beam flickered inches away, ready to slice through metal and flesh alike.

But before the torch could make contact, a single gunshot rang out. The deafening crack echoed through the room. The torch was knocked upward from Greeley's hand, spiraling, then down, slicing off his right hand in the process.

Greeley screamed, his eyes wide with disbelief as he stared at the cauterized stump where his hand had been. He collapsed to the floor, motionless, as if death had claimed him.

Jay stood in the doorway, smoke curling from his gun barrel.

Momentarily distracted, the cyborgs loosened their grip on Christopher. Seizing the opportunity, Christopher activated his photon cannons, unleashing a massive blast that vaporized the surrounding cyborgs. The few that remained were quickly dispatched, falling to the ground in smoking heaps.

As the dust settled, Jay slid the pistol back into its holster and made his way to Christopher, who was already back at Aurora's side. Christopher reinserted the interface pin without missing a beat and resumed his work.

"I figured you could use some backup," Jay said, his eyes flicking to Aurora. "That must be Project 24, right?"

Aurora smiled, sitting up now, her systems fully restored.

"Aren't you going to introduce me, Christopher?"

Jay raised an eyebrow.

"Christopher?"

"My name now," Christopher said.

Aurora got to her feet, slipping her arms around Christopher in a relieved embrace.

"This is my friend, police officer Jay Mauritius," Christopher said. "A good man to have around in a pinch."

Before Jay could respond, a crash echoed from the entrance. More mindless cyborgs poured in, their glowing red eyes cutting through the shadows like predators on the hunt. Dozens of them advanced, ready to strike.

"Run!" Christopher shouted.

Together, they sprinted toward the exit, Jay close on their heels.

One Final Mission

Without Zoe to guide him, Christopher took charge as they sprinted down the long, sterile corridor. The roar of the cyborgs closing in drowned out the sound of their footsteps. Christopher's sharp eyes scanned the narrow hallway ahead while Aurora and Jay kept close on either side, moving in sync with him.

The mechanical whirring behind them intensified, a reminder that time was running thin. They reached the hangar entrance and skidded to a stop in front of a massive, sealed gate. The cold, unyielding metal loomed before them. Christopher's fingers skimmed the lock, and his suspicions were confirmed. His jaw tightened as his hand morphed into a photon cannon.

"Cover me," he said.

Jay fumbled for his pistol. "I'm on it."

Christopher shot him a quick look. "Not you."

Aurora's arms shifted seamlessly, sleek photon cannons replacing her forearms. Her shots tore through the advancing cyborgs, each blast precise and lethal. Metallic bodies hit the floor, but reinforcements filled the space almost immediately.

Jay, momentarily taken aback, raised his pistol and fired until the clip emptied.

Christopher turned to the gate and unleashed a series of powerful blasts from his cannon. Sparks flew as the lock shattered, and the doors groaned open, revealing the vast hangar beyond.

Inside, they paused only for a second to take in the sight. The vast hangar seemed to stretch on for miles. Rows of drones, tanks, and missiles stood in eerie silence, waiting for activation. Sunlight streamed through the open hangar doors on the other end, casting long shadows across the floor and lighting up a clear path to their escape. Christopher moved without hesitation, sprinting toward a drone copter. He vaulted into the cockpit, his finger extending into a thin metal rod, which he jammed into the control panel. In seconds, the drone hummed to life under his command.

He jumped out and pulled Jay toward the drone. In one quick move, he secured Jay into the pilot's seat. His face gave nothing away, but his eyes held a determined focus as they locked onto Jay.

"Thank you, Jay," Christopher said. "For everything. But this is where we part ways."

Jay shook his head. "No way. Not now." He reached for the straps, trying to free himself.

Christopher pressed a small mag-ram into Jay's hand.

"This has everything. The truth. You have to get it to the right people."

Jay stared at the device, the weight of it far heavier than its size suggested.

"What about you?"

"We're on different paths now."

Christopher offered a faint smile, full of both warmth and finality. The drone lifted off, its engines roaring as it approached the hangar doors.

Their eyes met one last time, a silent goodbye before the distance swallowed Jay from view.

Christopher turned back to Aurora and took her hand. For a fleeting moment, the chaos around them—the clanking of cyborgs, the gunfire—seemed to vanish. They found calm in each other's presence, if only for the span of a pulse.

The enemy was closing in fast. Christopher's eyes darted to a stack of missiles in the corner of the hangar, then to the grenade he'd taken from Greeley's armory. Without a second thought, he pulled the pin and hurled it toward the missiles with deadly accuracy.

Outside the blast zone, Jay's drone landed behind the police barricade. Officers rushed toward him, pulling him from the cockpit just as the ground shook with a deafening explosion.

AICO South became a fireball, the shockwave knocking everyone to the ground. Smoke and debris filled the air as the building crumbled, and the sky darkened by the rising mushroom column of destruction.

Dazed but unscathed, Jay pushed himself up, his eyes fixed on the chaos ahead. Amid the falling debris, something caught his eye—a blackened, twisted object falling from the sky, crashing just yards away. Dread surged through him as he sprinted toward it.

It was a skull, metallic and charred by the blast. Jay knelt beside it, brushing away the ash to reveal its shape. It was Christopher's—at least, what was left of him.

Jay stood over the remains, uncertain whether this was indeed his friend or just another mangled cyborg. Christopher had always been the one to survive, defying death at every turn. Now, staring at the wreckage, Jay couldn't tell if this was the end of his friend or another escape in disguise.

Clutching the flash drive in his pocket, Jay knew one thing for sure—he had one final mission.

Epilogue

Log Entry: Final entry.
(Stored in holographic archive, text transcript below.)

My name is Jay Mauritius. I was a cop stationed in New Sinai, Washington Quadrant.

This is my final entry:

So, the rain's tapping against the windows, and everything outside is just this hazy blur. You know, it's the kind of day that slows you down, makes you think a little deeper. I'm just sitting here, watching the rain streak down the glass. It's quiet in here—warm, too. Lillian's in the kitchen, and Jennifer—she's eight months now—she's right here, playing, babbling away. It's... peaceful. Simple. So different from the life I used to live.

The TV's humming in the background, some report about Chancellor Bellwether dodging questions again. Same script, different actors. They think they can rewrite what happened, but the truth... doesn't disappear. They say you start believing it yourself if you tell a lie enough times. I've seen that happen, firsthand.

I glance down at my hands. They're scarred and worn, reminders of everything I've been through. These hands — they used to fight, used to do what needed to be done. Now? Now they hold my daughter. They protect what matters. My wedding band is just a simple reminder of what's real. These scars? They're more than just marks. They're the truth I carry with me.

And no lie can change that.

(pauses)

So, this buzz pulls me out of my thoughts—it's a message on my VoxLink. I check it, and it's from someone in Canada:

"Hello from Canada! You won't believe how beautiful it is here with all the snow. We both really miss you!"

I smile because I know exactly who that's from. It's funny, you know? Even in the middle of a storm, there's still some light.

(pauses)

I've seen enough lies to know when the truth is staring me in the face. This life I've built—it's real. The rain outside? It'll pass. It always does.

But this? This is what's worth holding on to.

Jay Mauritius, Sergeant. New Sinai Police Department.

The End

Appendix

The Governance of Quadrants
A Post-War Order

Hierarchy of Governance: The Power Structure of the New Superstates

An authoritative assessment of the four superstates' roles, strengths, and influence in shaping the nation's future.

—

President of the United States: The ultimate leader of the entire nation, responsible for all executive decisions, national defense, and foreign policy. The President's authority extends over all quadrants and states.

Vice President: The President's primary advisor and second-in-command, focusing on federal matters and representing the nation's executive power. The Vice President also plays a role in overseeing quadrant coordination alongside the Director of Quadrants.

Director of Quadrants: A high-ranking federal official tasked with managing the quadrants. The Director ensures the uniform application of national policies, coordinates between the federal government and the Quadrant Governors, and monitors inter-quadrant relations.

Quadrant Governors or Quadrant Chancellors: The essential authority in each quadrant, overseeing all the states within their jurisdiction. Chancellors have wide-ranging powers, managing quadrant-wide policies, resources, and military forces, and report directly to the Director of Quadrants.

State Governors: Since the original state borders remain intact, each state within a quadrant retains its Governor. State Governors manage their state's day-to-day affairs (education, healthcare, infrastructure, etc.) while adhering to the Quadrant Governor's and federal laws' directives. They are essential in ensuring local policies align with the broader quadrant and national goals.

State Legislatures: Each state would still have its Legislature, making decisions on state-specific issues, subject to approval or oversight by the Quadrant Governor to ensure coherence with national policies.

Regional Military Commanders: Each quadrant would have Regional Military Commanders, akin to *Generals*, who oversee the military forces within their territory. They coordinate with State Governors when necessary but report to the Quadrant Governor and federal military leadership. These commanders ensure the defense and security of their quadrant, maintaining military readiness and enforcing federal and quadrant-level security policies.

Quadrant Advisory Council: This council comprises state representatives, military leaders, and sectoral experts (such as agriculture, technology, or energy) from each state within the quadrant. They provide advice and insight to the Quadrant Governor on managing quadrant-wide initiatives and resource allocation.

State and City Administrators: State and City Administrators would continue to oversee localized governance at the city or county level. They ensure that quadrant-wide and state-wide policies are implemented effectively on the ground.

State Civilian and Economic Departments: Each state has its own departments dedicated to civil affairs, economy, law enforcement, and resource management. These departments coordinate closely with the Quadrant Ministries to ensure consistent policy implementation.

—

Territorial Overview of the Quadrants

Washington Quadrant (Northeast)

Capital: New Sinai

Territory: Encompassing the historic heart of the nation, including New York, New Jersey, Pennsylvania, Massachusetts, and the Washington, D.C. region. Extending westward to Ohio and Michigan for balanced resource distribution.

Identity: As the political and financial center, the Washington Quadrant is the pillar of strength and unity. Governance focuses on stability and progress through firm leadership, maintaining order within its diverse and industrious population.

Economy & Resources: A global leader in industry, finance, technological innovation, and government administration. New Sinai drives advancements in cyberinfrastructure and energy production, securing dominance.

Jefferson Quadrant (Southeast)

Capital: New Orleans

Territory: Spanning Virginia, the Carolinas, Georgia, Florida, Alabama, and Tennessee, with potential extensions into Texas or Mississippi for post-war resource control.

Identity: Defined by military strength and agricultural tradition, this quadrant emphasizes self-reliance and resilience. Strong values of defense and independence are rooted in its war-hardened history.

Economy & Resources: Leading in agriculture, natural gas production, and military-industrial capacity, the Jefferson Quadrant is a key food and energy supplier to the superstates.

Franklin Quadrant (Midwest/Great Plains)

Capital: Chicago

Territory: Covering the Midwest, including the Dakotas, Nebraska, Kansas, Oklahoma, Iowa, and Illinois, and possibly extending toward the Rockies. Great Lakes states like Wisconsin and Minnesota also fall within this territory.

Identity: Known as the agricultural and industrial backbone, the Franklin Quadrant is focused on self-reliance and internal stability. Post-war, this region prioritizes its own prosperity through agriculture and manufacturing.

Economy & Resources: A leading provider of agriculture, manufacturing, and renewable energy such as wind and solar. The quadrant supplies food and raw materials to the superstates, reinforcing its role as the nation's breadbasket.

Pacific Quadrant (West Coast)

Capital: San Francisco

Territory: Comprising California, Oregon, and Washington, with strategic extensions into Nevada and Arizona. Parts of the Southwest are also included to maintain economic balance and resource control.

Identity: The Pacific Quadrant is the most technologically advanced and culturally progressive. Its geographic isolation has fostered independence, making it a global hub for innovation and trade.

Economy & Resources: Driven by high-tech industries, entertainment, and Pacific Rim trade. Automation and cutting-edge technology dominate the economy, while California's agriculture still plays a significant role.

———

Power Dynamics of the Quadrants

Washington Quadrant: The political and administrative center, Washington Quadrant holds absolute authority over federal control, law enforcement, and technological superiority. It maintains national unity through advanced cyberinfrastructure and a robust security system.

Jefferson Quadrant: Known for its focus on independence and defense, the Jefferson Quadrant emphasizes military strength and traditional values. Its population is deeply committed to self-reliance and preserving their sovereignty.

Franklin Quadrant: Serving as the agricultural and industrial powerhouse, it is more internally focused, concerned with self-sufficiency and maintaining stability within its borders. It plays a crucial role in providing essential resources to the superstates.

Pacific Quadrant: Economically dominant through global trade and high-tech industries, it may challenge Washington's political power by leveraging its wealth and technological advancements. Its influence as a leader in innovation and international commerce is steadily growing.